First Limelight Edition February 1997

 Published by Proscenium Publishers, Inc., 118 East 30th Street, New York, NY 10016

Manufactured in the United States of America.

Library of Congress Cataloging-in-Publication Data

Sharff, Stefan.
The art of looking in Hitchcock's Rear window / Stefan Sharff.—
1st Limelight ed.
p. cm.

ISBN 0-87910-087-7
1. Rear window (Motion picture) 2. Hitchcock, Alfred, 1899-1980 — Criticism and interpretation. I. Title.
PN 1997.R353S52 1996
791.43'72—dc20 96-35372
CIP

THE ART OF LOOKING
IN HITCHCOCK'S
REAR WINDOW

Stefan Sharff

Limelight Editions
New York

To my wife Laura

Contents

PREFACE

MY GOAL in this book is to demonstrate that cinema art can be depicted as a work composed, not unlike an orchestral piece or a large painting. Regardless of the not totally unjustified lingering vicissitudes about the collaborative nature of filmmaking, one ought to expect that there exists a central entity, a "composer" who generates the design, the process and eventually the stylistic-aesthetic elements of a film. The design is most essential: from it comes the cinema language and tonality guiding all the moves to the most minute parts; every shot has consequences both forward and back, and all components play.

In the early stages of film history the phenomenal outburst of artistic talent and imagination (Griffith, Chaplin, Lang, Kuleshov, Eisenstein to mention a few) was similar to that of the early novel (Rabelais, Cervantes, Defoe, Sterne). In the case of cinema art, the film industry completely and globally took over with a profitable production of pulp, an avalanche not ever experienced by the other arts. Many masters, including some in Hollywood, nevertheless continued to extend the expressiveness of cinema language with a certain measure of success. Still, the large question remains how to overcome the damage of this almost total commercialization, the greatest consequence of which is the deterioration of taste.

This deterioration affects the providers as well as the consumers in a most deadening way: unavoidably it leads not only to the lowering of standards but, by sheer inertia, to the evaporation of aesthetic qualities. The presence of aesthetic forms is a *sine qua non* prerequisite of any art, and to an even greater extent when applied to cinema, a still-developing medium when looked at historically, albeit of titanic potentials. Contemporary films, even those above pulp level, are, in the opinion of the great French master Robert Bresson, not cinema but only theater on celluloid, leaning on actorial skills and

well-crafted dialogue. One of the ways to liberate cinema from the abyss of poor taste is to organize and analyze the works of the masters who, from way back, by leaps and bounds, kept enriching cinema language with unique cinesthetic forms. Those forms, as I have said already elsewhere, remain in an enigmatic cloud to many, reputedly only in the possession of the masters. One of those was Alfred Hitchcock, yet I hasten to add here that his so-called secrets are indeed quite accessible for those who learn how to look and see into his work: the art of looking is what this book is all about. I hope my attempts to illuminate the Hitchcockian language will be met with understanding.

Stefan Sharff
Professor Emeritus
Columbia University
August, 1996

1

THE ART OF SEEING, THE ART OF LOOKING

THE AIM of this study is to give a lucid exposition on the subject of cinema art, an art that is abundantly demonstrated in Alfred Hitchcock's *Rear Window.* I will attempt to identify the "materials" utilized by the master, and then proceed to a deeper level of analysis based on the principle of grammatization of his cinema language.

Why *Rear Window*? Among the dozen or so candidates for a classic, Hitchcock's 1954 *Rear Window* stands out for a number of reasons. It responds to the Pythagorean principle of aesthetics, demonstrating harmony, completeness and consistency. Also, *Rear Window* is a mainstream film, still from the Hollywood "Dream Factory," to use Elia Ehrenburg's title. Because it is mainstream, the film contains a core of solid normalcy. Also, and most important, the film overflows with authentic inventiveness and even avant-gardism, which in its subtle way extends the semantics of cinema. This film's narrative-pictorial material is purely cinematic in the way it explores the notion of looking. The language of images is sophisticated and complex, yet it appears to be so simple, like the extended silent sections—entirely image-dependent. In fact, almost 35 percent of the movie is silent, without dialogue.

When speaking about *Rear Window* one unavoidably touches upon the question of cinema art, which is not, I regret, a well-defined entity. There is no value-free way to speak on the subject; value is, anyway, a transitive term, changing with time. Yet, without a methodical theory it would be hard to decide what cinema art is!

In my previous attempts to systematize cinematic structures (Sharff '82, '91), [1] I arrived at a method of analysis that I shall also use in this text. Let the search for a definition of "Cinema Art" here bypass certain categories, like the Marxist, Freudian, sociological and populist kind, and concentrate on scrutinizing the film language, its quality, the peculiar image succession, its "magical" impact, its aesthetic value.

---

[1] *Elements of Cinema,* 1982, Columbia University Press.
Hitchcock's High Vernacular, 1991, Columbia University Press.

With a skillful use of cinema language, the connection to naturalistic representation is loosened sufficiently to allow for ambivalence. Cinema art transforms the photographic "mirror to reality" into a "cinema reality" by introducing rhythm and texture, so the whole modality becomes a world more dense and vibrant than the ordinary one around us. In no case can cinema art be a random collection of forms intuitively selected: *nolens volens,* they by necessity become a system of grammatical arrangements of cinesthetic structures. Those structures form part of the arena of magic experienced by all who are exposed to film viewing. What generates that magic? Essentially it is pieces of film spliced together in concert, in a sequence of meaning; just pieces of film, as Hitchcock described it in an interview with François Truffaut (see page 191).

Inasmuch as I shall be stating the case for *Rear Window* in many of its aspects, I have to be aware of the fact that most socially informed criticism in cinema is practiced by outsiders without identifiable expertise in cinema. My responsibility will be to inform and convince the reader that a number of forms are unique to cinema and, when skillfully manipulated by the artist, can result in a superb high vernacular.

In *Rear Window,* the geography, indeed the whole setting, may appear to be designed, at least on the surface, to serve a "Peeping Tom." However, like many surface observations, lightly spoken, this one too turns out to be false. What comes to light in the film is a relatively complex and peculiar phenomenon of human activity where the gravity shifts from the possibly mundane and banal to an essential perception of "the ineluctable modality of the visible."

The epicenter of the film is the notion of looking, observing and seeing across from the gazer, across from someone, "across. . . ." The window of protagonist L.B. Jefferies (James Stewart) is across from the other windows around the inner courtyard. Hitchcock robs the viewer in the audience of the faculty of simply seeing across without the guidance of a third person, the onlooker: Jefferies is the principal "seer," while we (the viewers) see him seeing—as well as what he sees. What seems to be limpid is at the same time opaque and odd: the relationship of the onlooker to the view across is complicated by

the bizarre notion that the movie theatre audience sees mostly what the protagonist chooses to observe. There are some exceptions when, on a few occasions, Hitchcock plants a surprise. At the outset of the film, for example, the floating camera, after exploring the general geography of the inner courtyard, comes upon the protagonist, who is sleeping. Thus, the audience is seeing (on its own) something the sleeping fellow, of course, does not. This plant takes on significance at a crucial scene in the middle of the film when the story is already in full swing: our protagonist, again asleep, misses seeing (during a previous five seconds) the unequivocal evidence for solving the murder case.

Such deviations temporarily destabilize us. During the bulk of the narrative, however, we get continuous confirmation that the onlooker is there to see for us. He is the anchor, in fact, he is the only one "across." It brings to mind a passage in the E.M. Forster novel *A Room with a View:* a murderous stabbing takes place on the Piazza Signoria in Florence and is witnessed by the story's two protagonists, the young Lucy and her future lover, George Emerson. When Lucy faints at the sight, George clutches her. The text describes the moment before her fainting: "Mr. George Emerson happened to be a few paces away, looking at her across the spot where the (murdered) man had been. How very odd! Across something?" The eminent critic Frank Kermode writes about this passage:

> This is a palpable disturbance of the narrative flow; it draws attention to itself as peculiar. We may reasonably expect in what follows to find some explanation of 'across...something.' But none is forthcoming ... What we have here is not so much a secret as secrecy...'[2]

In *Rear Window* something also remains at odds: we, the audience, are across these windows, the whole world is in front of us, across, to be seen. Hitchcock eerily makes his protagonist the one who controls the "acrossness": we see Jefferies, he guides us, we follow him.

---

[2] *Essays on Fiction,* Frank Kermode (Prologue, p. 13), Rutledge, 1983.

Consequently, the film operates on two basic modes: the normal realistic film in the protagonist's apartment, viewed in an ordinary, direct manner of audience versus the screen, and the world across (framed mostly in windows) viewed via the onlooker. Many films use the very useful choice of onlookers, though rarely with the same exclusivity as Hitchcock did in *Rear Window.* Half of this film is onlooker-controlled, and the dramatic core is totally dependent on it. Hitchcock's art, as always, is arranged in hierarchical layers. The across aspect is served as almost a subliminal effect, under Hitchcock's guidance as auteur: his method is to lay it out in silent-film fashion!

As mentioned above, one-third of *Rear Window* is a bona fide silent film with incidental music or sound effects; in addition, the actorial performances contain some silent film mannerism, mostly in long and medium-long shots. Later in the film, when the dramatic tension increases, the protagonist uses a pair of binoculars as well as a telephoto lens on his camera, affording him a closer look at the people he watches. This cleverly built-in realistic justification for changes in image size gives the filmmaker the needed flexibility and, as in silent films, we also start seeing occasional close-ups and medium shots, all on the same axis of view. The silent-film acting extends also to the onlooker, to his reactions, especially as he responds to a pantomime (from across) automatically with his own expressive gestures, also in pantomime.

Another layer in the Hitchcockian hierarchy of forms is his framing. Most of the viewed action is through the windows situated across the courtyard. Those innocuous windows become the frames for the screens of the small movies that are a part of the big film. The subjects are a community of people inhabiting the inner courtyard, in an urban setting of lower Manhattan—during the scorching heat of New York in summer. The principal members of this community with whom viewers become intimately familiar are: the young dancer in her two-window apartment, who in different stages of undress exercises, dancing almost continuously while doing chores; the musician, whose newly created song becomes the musical theme of the film—he has the largest window with a terrace; Miss Lonelyhearts, as the protagonist calls her, a sad figure going through many crises as

seen through her three-window apartment; a newlywed couple with their one small window; and most important, directly across, a four-window second-floor apartment occupied by a traveling salesman, Mr. Thorwald, whose drama becomes central in the film. The framing of the principal plots in the windows is creative, eccentric and somehow abstract. It is only at the end of the film that those windows and their oddness become demystified as the people who inhabit them come outside their "frames" (as in medieval bas-reliefs), literally out to meet their observer-onlooker in person.

Peeping innocently or, in fact, surreptitiously into peoples' windows smacks of voyeurism, and since film viewing as such is suspected to be the ideal vehicle for such a habit, *Rear Window* could be and was put into such a category. However, the subject of voyeurism should not dominate the analysis of this film. I shall return to the subject of voyeurism, briefly, in the summary. Jefferies, the protagonist, is somehow excused for his actions; in a wheelchair, his leg in a

cast for nearly six weeks with nothing to do, he looks. Peeping at the dancer, "Miss Torso" as he calls her, does provide a certain amount of sexual undertones; the rest is common observation born out of idleness. As the story progresses Jefferies suspects, with some reason, foul doings in Thorwald's apartment. Soon after, a passionate detective quest ensues. One should keep in mind that Jefferies is a photojournalist accustomed to nosing into other peoples' affairs. As a professional out to get his story he becomes an investigator of sort and, intrigued by a possible homicide, pursues it at the risk of his as well as his girlfriend's life, to the very end. In fact, he is tortured by doubts and ethical self-questioning yet at the conclusion is proven right.

The film, as created by Hitchcock, is concerned with cinema itself, with its unique way of looking and perceiving. To sharpen those faculties he incorporates an interesting limitation of space: the parameters in this film are tight. Jefferies' apartment is a smallish studio, with an unseen kitchen somewhere behind the bookshelf and a bedroom referred to but also never seen. The only interior door, besides the entrance, is to the bathroom, of which the inside is never seen in detail. The big window looks out to a courtyard, enclosed by the rear walls of apartment buildings and with only a narrow alleyway leading to the street. Occasionally, the Manhattan skyline is seen looming above these three-story buildings. The apartments with the windows across are small, mainly railroad flats, where one has to pass through one room to reach the next. Such limitations of space impose a strict discipline on the filmic concepts, where the paramount rule is precision. Part of that kind of rigor is the contrapuntal construction of the dramatic elements as well as the formal (graphic-camera-rhythm) ones. Dramatically, the story is arranged in trigger following release following trigger-release succession. Also contrapuntal are the two principal modes of camera bearings, the bountiful moving camera versus fragmentation, especially intense between the onlooker and the life he observes across. The imagery inside the protagonist's apartment is treated more conventionally, with elements of structure appropriate for scenes that are realistic and contain a fair amount of dialogue; they in turn are contrapuntal to scenes in the silent sections of the film with their dreamlike modality. Still, even

in Jefferies' apartment, Hitchcock uses his cinema language to cultivate the art of seeing, unique to this film: he trains the viewer by arranging the visual information, the combined memory of objects, in a way so they can be stored as familiar images. Once absorbed, those ultimately will be laid over new images and will form a continuum of a double reality: the immediate and the recalled. (A recall of oral information often used in films is another matter and another kind of intellectual activity.)

The ability to create such *familiar images* from the most commonplace or unremarkable items is the most knotty part of the language of cinema. It requires the highest degree of orchestration in framing, placement in the chain of shots and proper narrative strategy.

Consider the scene from the beginning of the film, two minutes after the titles have rolled (end of shot No. 5).[3] The camera finishes panning over the exterior walls with windows and eventually re-enters the window of the protagonist, whom we see in close-up sleeping and sweating profusely (in the 93°F heat). The camera, after a brief pause, continues exploring the interior of Jefferies' apartment; first we see that his leg is in a cast and he is in a wheelchair, then the camera floats over enlarged photos on the walls and his smashed 8 x 10 view camera. We learn that he is a photojournalist of some importance with a wide range of experience in war, sports, racing accidents, magazine covers, etc. The fact that this brief introductory biography of our protagonist is executed by a moving camera and in silent fashion, without any oral commentary, is important for its recall value and also as a stylistic imprint, since the film promotes the primacy of visual information and the merits of silent film. The fact that all we know so far about Jefferies—even his name inscribed on his cast—comes from the above visual biography makes those photos and items even more significant since they literally lay themselves over the next scenes when we see Jefferies talking and interacting with people; we cannot help but think of them while seeing him in action—a fair illustration of the term double reality.

---

[3] See Chapter 4 for a complete descriptive listing of shots from the film.

Another kind of recall, a "long distance" one and more abstract yet strangely gratifying when it occurs, takes place between an event in the very beginning of the film and one near its end. A comparatively minor business is shot No. 3, a cat walking along the edge of the garden (down from Jefferies' windows) and up a set of wide steps; the camera pans with the cat, follows it up the steps and then continues panning up, eventually leaving the cat out of the frame. The impression left is that the cat's ascent somewhat generated the camera movement up, a little ballet between cat and camera, as the panning continues to the windows across. We never see the cat again. Almost two hours later, in shot No. 603, Lisa and the nurse walk up the same steps on their daring expedition to seek proof of the murder, in itself a very suspenseful scene: the recall of the cat comes back with force despite the enormous time interval. In both examples the recalls are perhaps innocuous, not big happenings and, most likely, the perceptive motors are subliminal, yet they leave the viewer with a peculiar sense of fulfillment, a bit of a thrill.

Other types of recall are occasionally functional and quite predictable. Such are the three steps down to Jefferies' apartment. One hardly pays attention to them when Jefferies' visitors come and go. What's more, one barely remembers that there are any steps at all! However, at the end of the film, from shot No. 708 on, at the very peak of the drama when the suspected murderer Mr. Thorwald is entering the darkened room about to attack Jefferies, the viewer becomes unexpectedly aware that the assailant has the obstacle of three steps down before he can reach the protagonist. The recall is well-timed and accordingly functional. (A small anecdotal aside might be à propos: Hitchcock mentioned, in a conversation at Columbia University, that as art director on his first job in films in Germany, an early assignment he had was to design a stairway in a dramatic silent movie. From that point on, he told me, he was attracted to stairs, as is evident in his repeated usage of them.)

Even here in *Rear Window,* despite the cramped interiors, he still finds a role for three steps; for each step down the attacker faces an enormous explosion of photographic flash fired by Jefferies in desperate defense—each flash followed by a red afterglow overwhelm-

ing the entire frame. The scene is a good example of Hitchcockian suspense-making with purely cinematic means: intense fragmentation plus a pictorial chain that implies, rather than shows, raw violence in a vérité fashion.

The moving camera in this film is used in a flamboyant way, contiguously with fragmentation (representing the bulk of the style). Especially grandiose are the two panning shots of almost 360 degrees, one at the beginning of the film, the other at its closing. Hitchcock's special attention to symmetry as the absolute condition for aesthetic phrasing finds its crowning in the above dazzling, circular movements that bracket the film at both ends. However, the peculiarly interesting feature of those moving camera shots is the mode of slow disclosure inseparably built into them (since, as the camera moves, it comes upon images unforeseen, disclosing as it pans). Again it's a question of the art of seeing. Hitchcock's strategy is to make the viewers more attentive by sharpening their visual memory: information here circulates in silent form, without commentary. Most likely, free from clutter or oral data, the mind pays more attention to what it sees when the presentation is precise and contains unflagging aesthetic value. Moreover, the propensity for slow disclosure (as already cited) is in itself a source of gratification unique to cinema language. Also at work is the web of parallel actions, mainly between the silent scenes and the main drama. One should not forget that a far-reaching source of aesthetic gratification in this film is derived from the cunning humor woven throughout the fabric of the entire work, either in the form of the overt comedic persona (nurse Stella) or in the threads of subtle and whimsical farce during the silent sections as well as in the relationship between the two protagonists.

2

"REAR WINDOW:" SYNOPSIS OF THE STORY

TO HELP the reader recall the sequence of events, I present here a condensed and matter-of-fact synopsis of the actual continuity.

The film starts with an elegant, almost 360° panoramic camera sweep around an interior courtyard with garden. The roving camera-eye passes over a series of windows showing people starting the day and, finally, comes upon a close-up of protagonist L.B. Jefferies (James Stewart) asleep, sweating profusely, outdoor thermometer showing 93°. He is in a wheelchair, a full cast on his left leg. From the paraphernalia in his cramped apartment we surmise that he is a photographer for a leading magazine. All the above is in silent-film fashion, without any commentary.

Jefferies' large second-floor window looks out to the courtyard garden and the windows across. In his immobility he is killing time by innocently, and occasionally not so innocently, checking out his neighbors. What he sees are like silent 8mm movies, framed by windows behind which unfold dramas, or mock-dramas, as the case may be. Directly across from Jefferies' apartment is the window and terrace of the shapely and scantily dressed young dancer, by far the most enticing view for the sometimes lusty eye of Jefferies; he refers to her as "Miss Torso." One other neighbor is a composer, most of the time seen at his piano working on a new song. In the garden apartment lives a middle-aged, lonely woman whom Jefferies calls "Miss Lonelyhearts"; we shall see her attempting to find male companionship. Next to hers is the studio of a sculptress. Above, on the second floor, lives the traveling salesman, a big, bear-like man with a bedridden wife; theirs will be the dramatic core of the film. One couple has a small dog that they lower by rope, in a basket, to the garden. The dog will have a role in the drama. Near to Jefferies is a small studio, just rented to a young newlywed couple, who start their honeymoon behind a pulled-down shade that teases the imagination.

Jefferies' girlfriend Lisa (Grace Kelly) is gorgeous, but we are warned that there is a problem in their relationship. Jefferies confesses to his visiting nurse (Thelma Ritter) that Lisa is too much of a Park Avenue girl, rich and spoiled. The nurse, a humorously rough, almost

coarse, character, a vox populi in this film, repeatedly advocates that he get married to Lisa, and soon.

That evening Lisa arrives in grand style. She has ordered dinner to be brought to Jefferies' home, as a surprise, by a liveried waiter. Jefferies, in his usual ironic tone, thanks her: "The dinner is perfect, as usual." She loves him, and wants him to stay in New York to shoot fashion photography instead of going on assignment to Pakistan and other distant lands. He insists that his current lifestyle suits him best. They continue venting their differences while Jefferies watches the windows across: he sees Miss Lonelyhearts, pantomiming the arrival of an imaginary male visitor. On the second floor, the salesman is serving dinner to his sick wife. They argue; he is rough with her. Lisa interrupts this "peeping," she is critical of Jefferies' constant voyeurism. She leaves for home on a low note, and they seem near total breakup.

As the story progresses, Jefferies becomes suspicious of the traveling salesman: his wife seems to have disappeared. At night, during a heavy rainstorm, Jefferies sees the salesman leaving his apartment several times with the same heavy valise.

The next day, during a massage session with his visiting nurse, Jefferies shares his suspicions about the mysterious disappearance of the salesman's sick wife. The nurse willingly joins him in speculations of foul play. With the help of his huge telephoto lens, he sees, almost in close-up, the salesman wrapping a long knife and narrow saw in newspaper. A hint, a glimmer of an idea of a possible murder comes to mind.

Lisa, on her next visit, calls Jefferies "sick for looking so much into other peoples' homes." He defends himself, giving her the details of events in the salesman's apartment. In time Lisa too is drawn into the mystery and agrees to help. The nurse also collaborates. In addition, Jefferies calls in his friend, a New York City detective who, however, is pessimistic about the case.

Miss Lonelyhearts is preparing to go out on the town, apparently in quest of male company. Lisa enters Jefferies' apartment clad in a chic outfit, carrying an overnight case to show she can travel light, if called for. Miss Lonelyhearts, in the meantime, comes back with "a

date." Our protagonists watch as the young man becomes sexually aggressive. Eventually Lonelyhearts slaps him, the man leaves furious and she despairs.

The detective friend (Wendel Corey) informs them that he checked out all avenues concerning the wife's whereabouts, and in his opinion Thorwald is innocent of any wrongdoing. Jefferies himself begins to doubt, perplexed about the morality of his own probings. Then, suddenly, they hear a desperate shriek from outside. Down in the garden a little dog has been maliciously killed, its neck broken.

Lisa and Jefferies regain their confidence: the murder case is not yet solved. They see Thorwald washing the walls of his bathroom. The nurse, who also watches, remarks that "the murderer washes off the blood."

Jefferies writes Thorwald a provocative note: "What have you done with her?" Lisa volunteers to slip it under Thorwald's door, which she does with gusto. Jefferies, observing this operation from his command post by his window, is full of admiration for his "girl from Park Avenue." Thorwald, meanwhile, after reading the note, looks like a trapped animal. He takes a big drink of scotch and starts packing. First he unloads some jewelry from his wife's bag. Lisa conjectures that among those items might be a wedding ring, a key piece of evidence, since, according to her, no woman would leave it behind, even when she has to go to a hospital. Jefferies cooks up a bold scheme to get Thorwald out of his apartment for a short while. He calls Thorwald on the phone, and a real cloak-and-dagger exchange ensues between the observed and observer, their first contact with each other. Jefferies: "Did you get my note?" No reply. Jefferies proposes they meet for a business talk in the bar of the Albert Hotel "Right away." It works. Thorwald soon leaves the house, presumably for the hotel.

Lisa and the nurse run down to the garden and start digging in the corner where the dog used to sniff about. They find nothing. Lisa then undertakes a daring and potentially reckless move to enter Thorwald's apartment via the fire escape and through his window. Jefferies' protestations (which he mimics desperately from his

window) are of no avail. Lisa, in her full-skirted dress, boldly crosses the sill of the salesman's lair. Jefferies frantically calls his friend the detective, while Lisa starts looking around for the jewelry; she finds it, and sends Jefferies a smile from across. Suddenly, he sees the awesome bulk of Thorwald returning home. In panic, helpless, Jefferies calls the police. Thorwald, meanwhile, grabs Lisa by the arm, forcing her to her knees. He gets the jewelry back and he beats her; Jefferies screams silently, though Lisa's scream can be heard from across. The tension becomes unbearable. Just then the police arrive at Thorwald's corridor, relieving Jefferies.

Through his big telephoto lens Jefferies sees, in close-up, Lisa showing him the wedding ring she found and put on her own finger. Thorwald, standing next to her, notices her gestures and the wedding ring; his gaze wanders to the window across. He finally understands where his tormentor is. Jefferies' phone rings; no one is on the line, just breathing. He reaches for his flash equipment and a box of bulbs. After a long wait his door slowly opens; the ominous figure of Thorwald looms over him. Jefferies fires a flash bulb, a blinding light with a red afterglow. Thorwald tries to move forward. Jefferies fires three consecutive blinding salvos; Thorwald staggers at first, then bolts forward. He grabs Jefferies, chokes him and, after a struggle, pushes him out of the window. At that moment, the police arrive in the courtyard, with Lisa and the detective, just in time to partially break Jefferies' fall. The police overwhelm Thorwald; he confesses that he killed his wife and offers to take the detectives on a tour of the East River, where the body is. Fade out.

In the brief finale, in a grand symmetry to the beginning of the film, the roving camera visits our little "movie screens," windows behind which we see: Lonelyhearts, visiting the composer who plays her his new tune on a record player; the "torso" warmly greeting her husband, a small, chubby bespectacled GI; Thorwald's former apartment being painted; and a new dog being lowered in a basket. The camera eventually arrives at Jefferies, who is sleeping in his chair, as at the start of the movie, this time a smile on his face. As the camera pans we see that now both legs are in casts! Next to

him, on the couch by the window, lies Lisa dutifully reading a book on the Himalayas but, when she sees that Jefferies is asleep, she sneaks out a copy of Harper's Bazaar magazine and lustily leafs through it. End of film.

3

BRICKS AND MORTAR

HAVING REVIEWED the story of the film, we can now proceed to analyze the entire work, focusing especially on the impressive structural aspects. In the first shot after the titles (shot no. 2), the bamboo shades roll up and a camera dollies out of a window to an exterior wall with windows. (Incidentally, this dolly movement is in the opposite direction from the one that starts Hitchcock's film *Psycho:* there, the camera moves from the outside into a window and an office.) In *Rear Window* the movement signals forthwith that the film is outbound, looking out, also a lesson in viewing across. The moving camera picks up again (shot no. 3) and, after the previously mentioned walk of the cat, moves up and briefly travels over the windows on the other side, introducing to us the interior courtyard of the apartment building. Then, suddenly and quite unexpectedly, the still-panning camera re-enters the first apartment and comes upon a close-up of Jefferies,

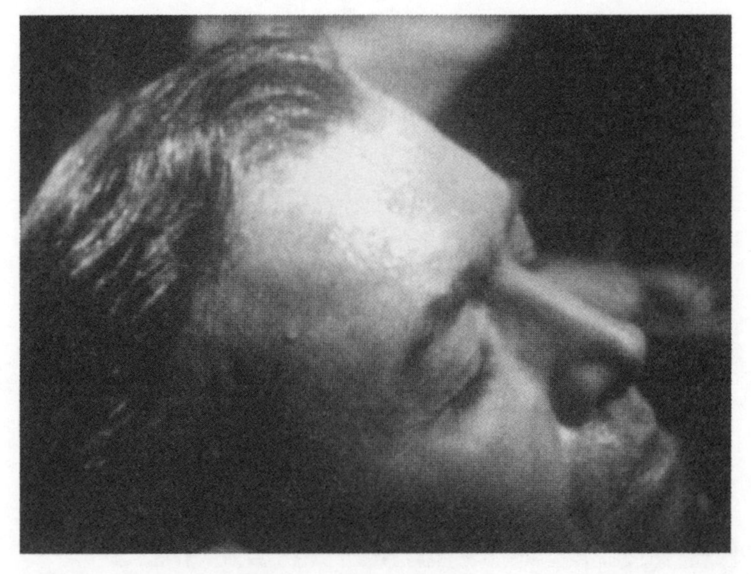

asleep in a reclining position close to his window sill. The camera's panning movement will be repeated soon after, and in greater detail. The surprise disclosure of Jefferies can be seen as a lesson in viewing: from now on the spectator will be on the alert for anything important that may unpredictably come into view whenever the camera is mov-

ing. On the aesthetic side, this introduction of the main character is executed with flair and a dash of originality. On top of the multifarious benefits of Hitchcockian forms, the circularity of the 360-degree pan is also important for it emphasizes the inner circle of the courtyard and its claustrophobic character. The next two shots (shot nos. 4 and 5), as already forecasted, are the repeated circular pans over the same territory; after a brief look at a thermometer showing 93°, we are introduced at a slower pace and more elaborately to several neighbors, namely the composer, via his bay window, who is in the middle of lathering his face; the pan continues, showing the people who sleep on the fire es-

capes to escape the oppressive heat, then again to the dancer's apartment as we see her prancing around from one room to the other, over to the garden level and the narrow alleyway to the street and up to a replayed disclosure of the protagonist's face, still asleep.

The panning movement is not finished yet: after a brief pause, the camera continues exploring the interior of our protagonist's apartment, starting with the cast with L.B. Jefferies inscribed on it,

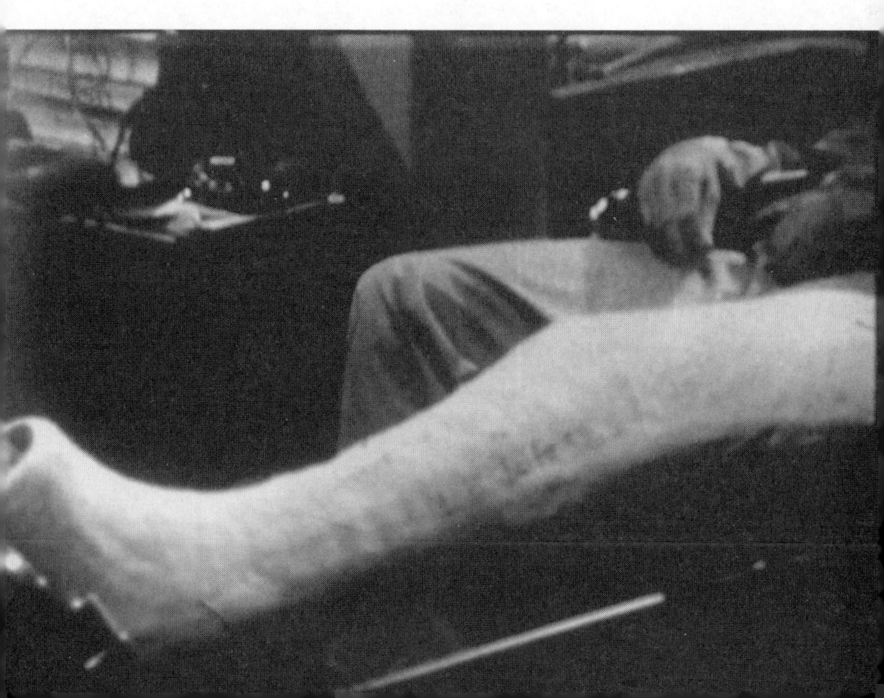

then the walls with photos as already described: his visual biography. Next the camera stops on a stack of magazines with a cover photo, most likely by Jefferies. At this point, after almost two minutes of panning, the curtain comes down unexpectedly, in the form of a fade-out, an omnipotent signal used abundantly in this film for closures, deletions and passages of time and which contributes to the film's mysterious air.

By now we are almost three minutes into the movie. The most distinctive strategies so far are: the cumulative layering of information, the slow disclosures, the formation of familiar images that will eventually weave themselves into the fabric of the rest of the film and the maverick introduction of the sleeping protagonist twice, all in silence. Still to come are the rest of the players in the numerous plots and subplots, and, most important, the looking across. Until now, while the protagonist sleeps the audience does the looking objectively on its own. As for the community of neighbors, we meet only the composer (with a cameo by Hitchcock as his visitor) and, more extensively, the sexy dancer. So far, after the preliminaries, the narrative is progressing slowly, with an accent on humor.

After the fade-in we find Jefferies shaving. The silent section has ended (loud street noises are heard in the background); he picks up the ringing phone and talks to his boss at the magazine. He also starts looking out through his window. Two women are on the roof terrace, partially hidden behind a short wall, throwing over the clothing they have taken off, most likely for nude sunbathing (shot no. 7). Jefferies is still on the phone and will continue to be so for the next 24 shots, at the same time looking out and watching. A helicopter (shot no. 9) lowers itself over the roof for a better view of the girls. Jefferies reacts to what the helicopter pilot might be seeing. This is a peculiar situation: the view on the roof is neither Jefferies' nor ours, only the pilot's. Still, Jefferies smiles; he understands, and we react accordingly, to his dictate. Then the onlooker, Jefferies, lowers his gaze to an already familiar location, the dancer's apartment. She continues her dancing while performing morning chores (shot no 11). Jefferies is amused. We, the viewers, follow his reaction, his smile; the next series of five shots of the dancer and five

shots of Jefferies watching her are already establishing the looking across that is so central to this film.

His phone conversation is all business with a dash of salt, humorous in tone and confirming what we, more or less, know about Jefferies' work, his accident (the smashed view camera, the photo of an overturned racing car) and his desire to get back to work; talking about his boredom. He even says: "Nothing to do but watch my neighbors."[1] He again changes the direction of his gaze: he sees a sculptor, a middle-aged, corpulent woman, who reacts to a noise from outside and turns her face (shot no. 21). Jefferies, still on the phone, again changes his gaze. We wait to see: the composer is at the

---

[1] See Chapter 4 for a complete dialogue.

piano, and he also reacts to the same outside noise before going back to his piano to correct notes on a pad by the stand. (Thus, an aural unity of space is established.) Jefferies, still on the phone, implores his boss (shot no. 24): "You have to get me out of here or else I'll get married and all will. . . ."

Back to the composer, who plays a tune. Jefferies anew changes his gaze; scanning to the left, he sees the four windows across, on the second-floor apartment of, as we learn later, Mr. Thorwald (Raymond Burr), the traveling salesman and his ailing wife. We see the salesman's heavy bulk entering the apartment from the corridor and walking to the middle window. He takes off his jacket, the camera pans with him as he proceeds to the next room where his wife is in bed. On the soundtrack off screen we hear Jefferies' conversation: "If I get married I won't be able to go any place anymore," and the reply: "It's time you get married, before you turn into an old and bitter man." By now (four and a half minutes into the film), slowly and unsuspectingly we arrive at the inner stage—the salesman's apartment—from where, later, the main drama will radiate, while the other windows and their inhabitants will provide the subplots.

It would be useful at this point to look at the architecture of the silent films within the windows. To start, the camera usually encompasses in a long-shot view three windows at a time. Since those will make the little screens very small (like little monitors in a television studio), Hitchcock soon switches to closer views of two windows at one time, justifying it by having Jefferies roll his wheelchair closer to the window or, as happens at one point, Jefferies leaning forward to see better. The characters, when they walk from room to room, are followed by the camera movement from window to window. Such changing of rooms and the widened scene within them are the only variants available to the director. Later in the film, when binoculars and long lenses are used (by Jefferies), the options of subject size will increase considerably.

Note that Hitchcock prefers to validate, realistically, such options and choices to help ease in the "silent films" without turning attention to them as such. Because the people inside those windows are far across, we accept the fact that we don't hear their conversations or any other noises except the loud ones, such as the composer's piano music or shouts in the garden. However, we do see them react to noises of the city, like in the previous case of the composer and the sculptor. Jefferies' phone conversation goes on while he watches and becomes, at times, a contrapuntal commentary to what he sees. Later in the film his comments, as well as those of his companions, while looking, often are synchronous with what they see.

In shot no. 29 Jefferies is looking at the salesman Thorwald; for the first time he sees just two windows filling his range of view. Thorwald is walking to the bedroom, his sick wife sits up in her bed, they argue and Thorwald dismisses her with a shrug.

In the next shot Jefferies finishes his phone conversation, hangs up the receiver, and eagerly goes back to his looking when he notices an argument is brewing across. In shot no. 31 Thorwald shouts at his wife, throws a magazine with fury and walks out to the next room. Curiously enough, while Jefferies notices (in shot no. 32) the serious discord in the Thorwald family, Hitchcock is not ready to pursue it yet—a release is needed after the hint of a trigger. This he provides in a hilarious way: Jefferies has an itch inside his cast; a long wooden Chinese back-scratcher comes in handy; he inserts it inside his cast and, with relish, scratches away. This comical interlude lasts 32 seconds (in silence), the longest-duration shot since the last fade-in.

The next 10 shots reaffirm that Thorwald is choleric: Jefferies observes him coming out to the garden and attending to the rose bushes, while the sculptor, who is by now lounging on her chaise, alerted by Thorwald's activity, comes over to the fence and pantomimes to

him to stop digging. Thorwald, annoyed, shouts at her; after a few exchanges he tells her to shut up—loud enough to be heard above the street noises. (This is the first lip-sync breach in the silent film.) The sculptor, upset and hurt, walks away. We see Jefferies three times during those 10 shots, for two seconds or less at a time. His tenacious looking is interrupted by the arrival of the visiting nurse (Thelma Ritter), another release, comic to be sure, after a trigger (eight minutes into the film.) The nurse will from now on provide the film's comedic succor with her constant talking, her coarseness

and homespun philosophizing. With her arrival—she sticks forthwith a thermometer in his mouth—life becomes more animated in Jefferies' apartment.

As was the case with the looking, this phase also starts slowly with new information about the limping liaison Jefferies endures with his girlfriend, Lisa. We get the lay of the land on that score quickly, the nurse being a strong champion for his promptly marrying Lisa. His bone of contention seems to be that Lisa is a Park Avenue girl, interested in dresses and leisure, not fitting into his lifestyle of a globetrotting photo reporter. A narrative pattern appears: new information is coming in tersely, still to be repeated and elaborated upon in later scenes. The ebb and flow of Jefferies' relationship with Lisa is pivotal to the story and runs parallel with the looking across. The above scene has 38 shots, seven minutes in length, and contains 17 shots in the separation mode (singles) while the preparatory six shots include some camera movements and a busy and cogent mise-en-scène. The separation incorporates most of the dialogue and singularly original framing: the nurse is setting up for a massage, with Jefferies lying on a platform directly facing the camera. In the singles: A, B, A, B, of the separation we see (A) Jefferies' face and the nurse's arms only—her head is out of the frame; in (B) the nurse's head and arms are seen, while only the top of his hair can be seen. A rather

unorthodox composition—an absolute taboo as per standard Hollywood usage—yet it is genuinely humorous and in harmony with the tone of the scene.

After the massage the nurse disappears to the kitchen to prepare a sandwich for him, saying: "I'll put some common sense into it. Lisa

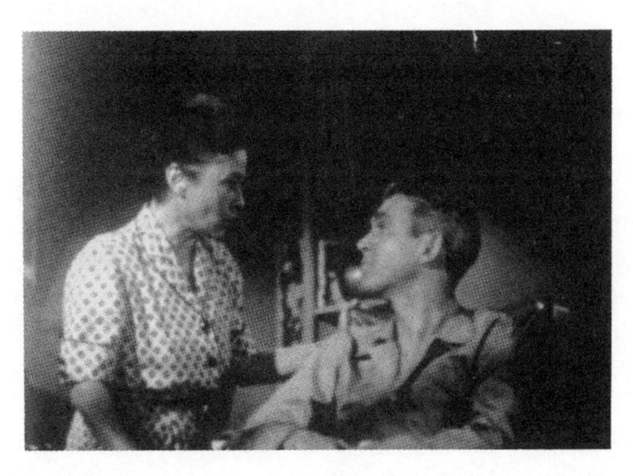

is the girl for you—marry her." Jefferies returns to his interrupted looking, and briefly sees the salesman leaving the garden with his tools, the sculptor asleep on her chaise longue and then, for two seconds, the dancer through her small window as she combs her hair; finally, reacting to the noise of a squeakily pulled up window, Jefferies looks and sees in the small window nearest his a young couple straight from a wedding getting their keys to the new apartment. Characteristically, after a short review of the already familiar inhabitants and after concluding the action that started before his nurse's arrival (the salesman in the garden), we are introduced to the "newlyweds." He sees, and we too with his help, a charmingly pantomimed replay of a ritual: kissing, carrying the bride over the threshold, and finally pulling down the shade. It is worth noting that a slight change of angle on Jefferies from a low medium close-up to an eye level medium close-up (in shot no. 74), when he leans over to see better, leaves the impression that we the viewers see the newlyweds closer than before even though the framing of their little window does not change at all. Jefferies is seen four times during the

captivating pantomime and his reactions are a good guide to the innuendos: embarrassed when they kiss, understanding when they pull down the shade. Just before the shade is pulled down the nurse reappears, sandwich in hand, admonishing Jefferies by calling him a "window shopper." The scene comes to a symmetrical closure with a fade-out.

The newlyweds' window shade becomes from now on a new blank white screen with imaginary action and meaning of its own, occasionally lifted and closed again.

The fade-in brings us to the evening of the same day—still in the introductory part of the film (by now 15 $^1/_2$ minutes). We shall observe this time objectively, without the help of Jefferies; the elaborate presentation of Lisa contains two slow disclosures as well as a symmetry. The latter repeats the camera pan over the windows, starting with the composer's, then the dancer's, both dressed for an evening out; above the building we see the Manhattan skyline at sunset, and the camera continues moving past the alleyway, eventually reaching Jefferies' windowsill. He is sleeping again. A shadow moves over his face, then a close-up of Lisa, the source of the shadow. She moves in closer; cut from her shadow to her face and once more to the shadow; Jefferies begins to wake. Lisa moves in and reaches the extreme close-up size. Suddenly a cut (shot no. 87) to a two-profile close shot of Jefferies and Lisa moving in closer to each other; finally they touch lips, a gentle kiss, and she retracts an inch; they talk in whispers. The most striking and original aspect here is Lisa's approach, at first forward, then, at the two-profile stage, horizontal. This is a radical shift, disconcerting and startling, yet eventually gratifying. (And pointing to Hitchcock's curiosity about the phenomenon of the human profile.)

The presentation of Lisa continues; after exchanging a few repartees, Jefferies asks, "Who are you?," upon which Lisa retreats from the frame. The camera suddenly veers from the profile to a frontal view of Jefferies (a resolution of the profile, perhaps). The energy generated by this camera movement finds repose in the next shot: Lisa, in a most amazing Hitchcockian mise-en-scène, presented with flair, answers Jefferies' question. In the darkish, cramped quarters (in a medium-long shot) she turns on the light in a large vase lamp

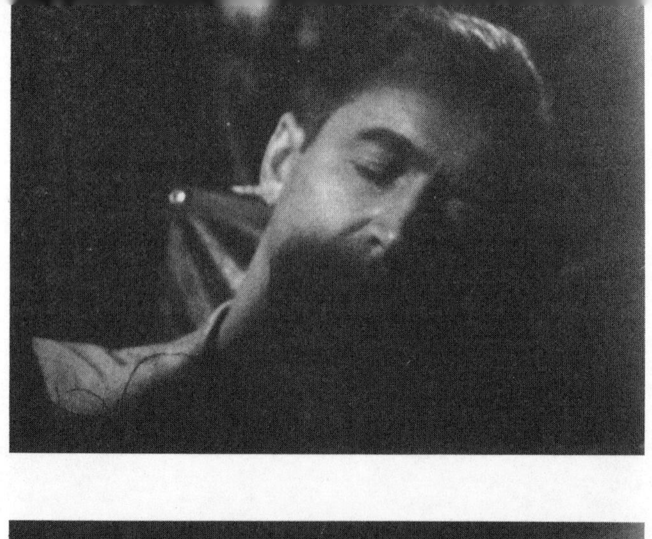

saying, "Lisa"; then she glides over as the camera pans with her to the next lamp standing on a table, turns it on, likewise saying, "Carol," and finally sails over to the other corner of the room, switches on a third standing lamp, announcing graciously her last name, "Freemont," all the while posing like the finest model, in her daz-

zling skirt of the latest Parisian fashion. By now she is already in a long shot. What follows is part of an 18-shot separation: Jefferies is almost sarcastic in his irony, occasionally pulling her leg, pretending admiration while he actually puns and quips. In the midst of it Lisa comes up with a grand surprise: a dinner from "21," delivered home by a liveried waiter, with wine and all. Jefferies, at first bewildered, concedes that such is her style.

While the dinner is kept warm in the oven, they drink wine and Lisa comes to the point: she would like Jefferies to leave the magazine, stop traveling and settle in New York, promising him lucrative contracts in the fashion industry, etc. Jefferies will not hear of it, saying: "Can you see me driving to the fashion salon in my combat boots, in a Jeep, with a three-day beard? Would that make a hit?" An impasse is reached. We were prewarned of this during the massage scene with the nurse, a typical example of Hitchcock's strategy of layering information at first in a terse from to be followed by a dramatic elaboration. Lisa walks away to fetch the dinner that is warming

in the oven. Jefferies turns to his window to look—to escape, perhaps, from his troubles.

Next, the resumed looking will yield an introduction to another neighbor, Miss Lonelyhearts, who lives on the ground floor and begets the important subplot that will weave in and out for the rest of the film, parallel to the other plots. We shall observe how skillfully Hitchcock uses that parallelism for purposes of deletion, or delay, or to heighten suspense, and how he deepens the penetration of those subplots (the source and consequence of looking) into the private and civic life of his protagonist.

Jefferies at first glances over the salesman's windows, seeing the wife sitting up in bed; a fast camera moves down to the window of Lonelyhearts, who is fixing her hair; back to Jefferies looking (1 sec.), then to a 19-second pantomime of Lonelyhearts, the camera following her as she walks between the window of her apartment picking up a bottle of wine on the way and returning to her dining room to light a couple of candles. Jefferies gazes intensely. Next, Miss Lonelyhearts walks past three windows to her entrance door, invites in an imaginary caller and leads him back to the dining table and bids him to sit down (29 sec.). Jefferies observes with interest. Lisa is partially seen, preparing to serve their dinner (3 sec.). Lonelyhearts greets her shadow guest, offers her cheek for a kiss (7 sec.). Jefferies looks, then checks if Lisa is around—she is gone again. Lonelyhearts serves the wine to her "guest" (5 sec.). Jefferies smiles (3 sec.). Back to Lonelyhearts filling the other glass with wine (2 sec.). Jefferies lifts his wine glass (2 sec.). Lonelyhearts picks up her glass, saluting her phantom companion (3 sec.). Jefferies too salutes her from his window (2 sec.). Lonelyhearts sips her wine (4 sec.). Jefferies also sips his wine (2 sec.). The final cut is to Miss Lonelyhearts, her glass in hand, looking sadly at the empty seat, finally collapsing, her arms stretched out on her table (19 sec). Cut to a shot of the two onlookers; Lisa is now seen also watching, next to Jefferies. They both sympathize with Lonelyhearts.

As the above scene shows, Jefferies makes a tentative attempt (with his wine glass pantomime) for an ephemeral contact with Miss

Lonelyhearts; a precursor, planted by Hitchcock, of the future, more weighty, linking of the seer with the seen.

Since this is the first full-fledged subplot in the film, with its own dramatic content, it would be legitimate to ask what exactly makes this silent episode so attention holding, even riveting? The easy answer would be all the ingredients, every moment of it, even the context (its placement, also its dire emotional content). Still, a few of the cinematic elements can be focused upon: Lonelyhearts walking from room to room adds mobility to what is basically an arrested action within a confined space; the horizontal camera pan trailing her progress, showing her through the windows, diverts the viewer from the absence of camera angles; finally, the rhythmical interruptions created by the close-ups of Jefferies' face as he watches impose a change in both size and presence, spilling over into the little screens like an after-image, a testimony that they are seen. The latter is important, since the viewer of the film is learning to distinguish between images seen by the onlooker (Jefferies) and those that are not, a distinction singular in this film. At present there are two onlookers, Lisa having joined Jefferies on the way to and from the kitchen; again they exchange a few cutting remarks.

It is worth noting that the Lonelyhearts subplot is planted in the middle of a serious domestic crisis between our protagonists. As detailed in the description of the next group of shots (from 134 to 157) it is apparent that two major crises are actually in progress and juxtaposed ironically: the one between the elegant Lisa and Jefferies versus the one brewing in the household of the traveling salesman and his ailing, annoying wife. The latter, as we know, becomes the film's major drama. Clustered in between is a fleeting look at the newlyweds' still-shaded window, then a longer gaze at the dancer's little party (a release after the tension of the Lonelyhearts incident), followed by the composer's studio, where we hear him playing his new, romantic tune. In a circular fashion the camera brings us back to Lisa and Jefferies sitting down to their sumptuous dinner. Characteristic of his mood, Jefferies finishes the scene with a cutting remark that the dinner is perfect. . . as usual.

Such bunching together of the several subplots around crisis situations is by now becoming the pattern, even though it may appear as a routine and random review of Jefferies' domain. Hitchcock's strategy is precise and cunning. The critical situation leading to an open conflict between the salesman and his wife is presented in a complex manner. The scene is of paramount importance, in fact it is the last time we see his wife before her presumed murder. The language is finely tuned in anticipation of the significant events to come. First, there are the innovations in framing, however innocuous: as Thorwald serves dinner to his wife (shot no. 143) he is framed in one window only (the bedroom); after shots of Jefferies watching comes the shot (no. 147) that covers two windows simultaneously.

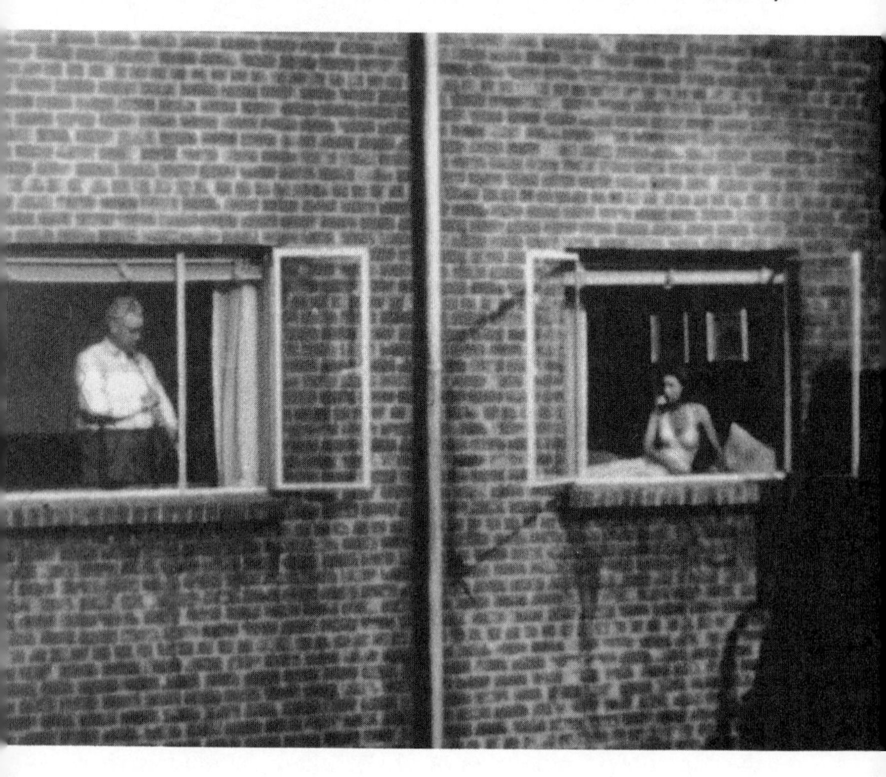

In the left one, the sitting room, Thorwald is dialing the phone, glancing occasionally to the next room. Reassured that his wife is peacefully eating, he pours himself a drink, and sits down in an easy chair for a covert phone conversation (presumably with his clandestine lover). In the right window, meanwhile, his wife slowly puts aside her dinner tray, eases herself stealthily out of bed and starts tiptoeing towards the wall to overhear her husband's conversation. This is clearly a noteworthy change in framing as the onlooker sees two actions simultaneously on two "small screens" (windows with a wall space between them). A similar instant parallelism is played out on a higher level of suspense at the end of the film, when the police are seen in one window and Thorwald molests Lisa in the other.

At present in the next shot (no. 148), Jefferies reacts with heightened interest, leaning over his sill as if to hear Thorwald's phone conversation from across, generating the next framing of one window only, in a closer shot, as Mrs. Thorwald sneaks closer to her husband. The camera follows her to the wall space between the windows, where she is hidden from view. The magic of the hidden action, so unique to film, is at work. Soon we see her hands penetrating the space on her husband's side. He notices her, drops the receiver and walks towards her. She laughs nervously. A pantomime "war" breaks out, yet it's mostly hidden from view as both of them by now enter the wall space between the windows; he may have struck her; eventually, they both emerge into the bedroom, and the camera pans with them. He shouts with passion and, finally, with a "to hell with you" gesture storms out of the room.

The next innovation, a small one but indicative of Hitchcock's resourcefulness of visual devices, is the reflection of Thorwald in the open windowpane, set at a certain angle, mirroring images from inside the room, sometimes of figures partially hidden in the above mentioned space between the windows. Again, such devices are used with great dramatic force later in the climactic parts of the film.

Next, Jefferies, after pondering what he has seen, directs his gaze to the composer's studio (shot no. 151), where the musician is playing his new tune to a visiting friend, Hitchcock himself, in one of

the frequent cameo appearances he makes in his films. This action brackets the end of the Thorwald subplot—in the beginning of which was the newlywed's window.

We are back in the midst of the Lisa-Jefferies intense confrontation, involving an irreconcilable discordance about their future, and they are on the brink of breaking up. Again, the cinematic format is similar to the one in the first part of their argument before the dinner: Hitchcock again uses the crescendo principle by starting with a 19-shot salvo of over-the-shoulder shots (from Lisa to Jefferies and vice versa), followed by 16 forceful separation shots (singles) as the argument gets harsh, in earnest. The over-the-shoulder shots (nos. 158 to 176) are arranged with foresight, once more confirming how determined Hitchcock's blueprint and execution is: Jefferies is shown in three-quarter profile, Lisa is reclining on a narrow padding by the window. The same arrangement will be repeated in the very last shot of the film, albeit with a moving camera: an extraordinary symmetry is achieved by placing the characters in exactly the same positions yet in converse moods and circumstances, the former in the midst of a rift and the latter at a time of harmony. Considering the many symmetries Hitchcock creates in this film, it is admirable how faithful he is to the St. Augustinian theorem that art without symmetry does not exist.

After the over-the-shoulder shots the crisis between the protagonists is cresting. Lisa gets up and moves around, gathers her things and, reminiscent of her arrival, puts on her long gloves. The dialogue gets rough, almost stormy. Finally, when she is at the door, Jefferies draws back a bit, mumbling: "When am I going to see you again?" (shot no. 191). She: "Not for a long time. . . ." then, after a pause, "Not until tomorrow. . . ." She leaves. The separation is never resolved since we do not see them again in the same frame. Jefferies is left alone to agonize and he is given a considerably longer duration shot (21 sec.).

He starts looking out his windows again. The camera moves along the apartments across; suddenly, a sharp scream reverberates in the courtyard, correlated with a quick camera pan to the left (shot no. 195). Jefferies reacts to the noise. Again a sudden fade-out cuts the

scene short, while the fade-in indicates only a short deletion until later the same night. Note the important change in rhythm: the next four scenes are short and the fades once more indicate only short time deletions.

We find Jefferies sleeping in his wheelchair (shot no. 197). It starts raining. Jefferies slowly wakes up and sees how the people on the fire escapes are scrambling to gather their bedding. Jefferies smiles. The scene, with its silence and humor, is strongly contrapuntal to the previous stormy exchange with Lisa. The couple on the balcony across push their mattresses through a window and dive in to avoid the heavy rain. In the small window in Thorwald's entrance hall he sees the traveling salesman, in rain gear, locking his door and leaving. Jefferies wonders; he looks down to the alleyway; the salesman, valise in hand, is crossing the street. Jefferies (shot no. 208), curious, checks his wrist watch. It's 1:50 a.m. Fade-out. Then, fade-in on the same watch showing 2:35 a.m. The salesman is seen coming back with the same valise but apparently a lighter one (trigger). Jefferies wonders what he is up to. Next, a release: Jefferies, attracted by a light in the composer's studio, sees him entering in a state of intoxication, tossing from wall to wall, trying to play the piano, hurling his papers to the floor. Jefferies is amused, tries to settle back to sleep, but he sees the salesman leaving anew (trigger) with his heavy valise, crossing the street, while it thunders and pours outside. Jefferies marvels, puzzled. Fade out.

Again, a short deletion. Later that night: Jefferies sleeps, wakes up, looks across. The salesman's windows are dark, the shades down, the lit corridor is empty. Jefferies takes a drink (shot no. 225). He checks the alleyway, and only sees passing cars on the street; he looks up to the dancer's apartment (release). She has just entered, apparently back from a party, judging from her dress. She's struggling at the door to prevent an unwanted companion from entering. She succeeds. Jefferies looks back at the alleyway to see the salesman coming back with the empty valise. The camera pans as Jefferies turns his line of vision, passing the dancer's window to the corridor: Jefferies, desperately needing sleep, watches with diffi-

culty as the salesman unlocks his door. The dancer's window goes dark, as does the salesman's apartment (shot no. 232). Fade-out.

Fade-in later same night. Jefferies in close-up is sleeping, then the camera pans away from him over to the salesman's windows (the crucial objective shot). In his corridor *we see* Thorwald in the company of a middle-aged woman in black ready to leave; camera pans back to Jefferies' window where he is still sleeping. This shot (no. 233) lasts 27 sec. and is the last and shortest of the series of four scenes bracketed with fades. As previously discussed, this is the scene where Jefferies blunders by sleeping—if he had been awake he probably would have had evidence that the woman in black is not Mrs. Thorwald. Evidently the change of rhythm is designed to coincide with the narrative turn of events. The suspicion of murder as well as the detective work pertaining to it will begin soon.

The next fade-in acts like a normal deletion. It is the next day. We see objective shots, without the onlooker: exterior day long shot (no. 234), the ground-level studio of the sculptor next to the alleyway. She is putting some finishing repairs to her abstract piece, a working man is delivering an ice block, he exchanges a few words with the sculptor, the camera pans up to the dancer's window. We see her prancing about as usual, the camera continues panning to the fire-escape platform where a new member of the cast is introduced, a little dog, who is lowered in a basket down to the garden. Then, unexpectedly, the camera swings to the left, ending inside Jefferies' room, in the middle of a massage session, the panning ends with a deep, technically very skillful camera penetration via the window into Jefferies' apartment.

We find him talking to the nurse about his discovery of the salesman's comings and goings during the stormy night. In a sense, the position of the viewer of the film is now strengthened since we know something—about the lady in black with Thorwald—that our onlooker does not. This scene contains the predictable elements of comical release, thanks mainly to the nurse. It lasts 1

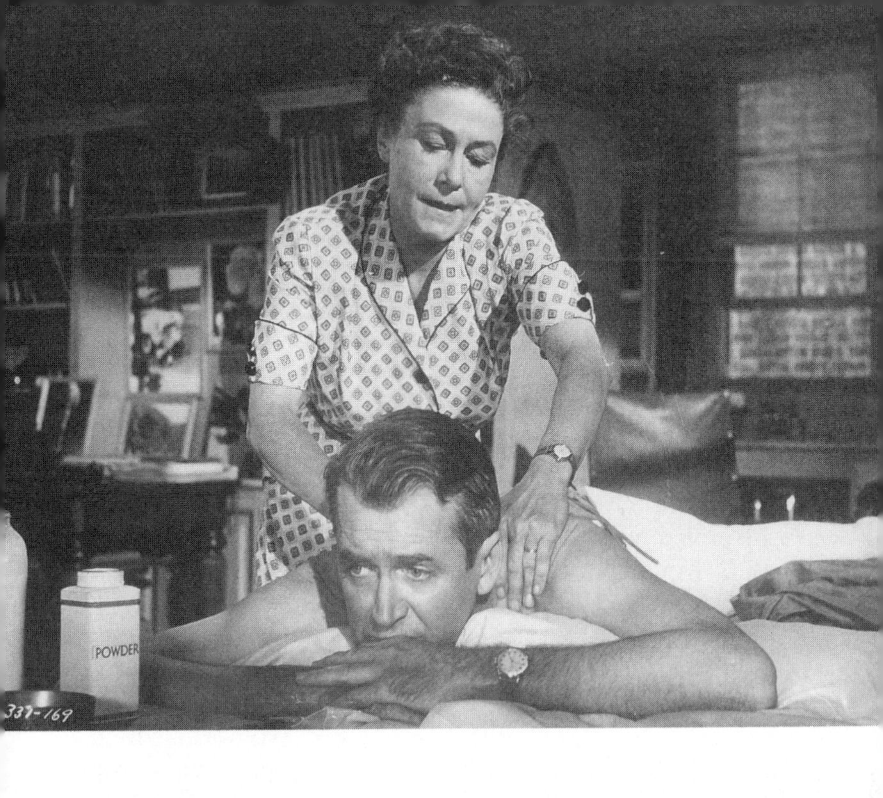
POWDER
337-169

min., 47 sec., without cuts. The objective viewing ends when, after the massage, the nurse and Jefferies look across. The salesman is at his window, gazing down. To Jefferies he looks like "a man afraid that someone is watching him." He and the nurse watch intensely. It turns out that Thorwald is watching the little dog smell out the rose bushes. The owner calls the dog back, he obeys and jumps into the basket. Mr. Thorwald is now busy cleaning his valise. Jefferies asks the nurse, who is ready to leave, to hand him his field glasses. Jefferies looks through them, the camera moves in, and we see a reflection of

the windows across in the binoculars. We finally see closer shots of Thorwald cleaning his display case (the same valise he was carrying in and out the night before). Jefferies moves his wheelchair back, afraid he might be seen. He needs greater magnification, so he reaches out for his big telephoto lens and his camera. In silence, he attaches the lens to his camera with the exactitude and even pedantry of a professional, for 1 min., 5 sec. (in real time), a typical delaying action for things to come, as well as a quiet release before the trigger. To be sure, the first item he sees (shot no. 253) with the big lens is a close shot, via the small kitchen window, of the salesman wrapping in newspapers a long and narrow saw and a sizable knife, then taking the package into the next room. Several times we see Jefferies lowering the heavy lens and resting it on his knee, then back to closer shots of Thorwald taking his thick glasses off, stretching and finally lowering himself into a couch next to the window. "The medium is the message," to use Marshall MacLuhan's famous phrase: the lens technically extends the flexibility of the cinema language by adding close-ups to the "silent films" in the windows. The last shot in the scene, before a fade-out, is of Jefferies, in a telling close-up, in deep thought: an idea seems to be born in his mind—a first visible suspicion of an alleged murder.

As with the fade-in in the outgoing scene, the fade here is followed by what appears to be also an objective viewing, without the help of the onlooker. The camera is routinely reviewing the "domain": it starts with a thermometer at 82°, moves on to the composer's studio as he scrubs the floor, trying in between to play a few notes, then to the people on the fire escape readying their bedding for a night under the stars, then to the dog owner whistling, panning down to the garden where the dog jumps into the basket, the camera passing the dancer's studio and the sculptor—eventually penetrating into Jefferies' window where, unexpectedly, we find him and Lisa, *in flagrante*, passionately kissing. Note again that the camera panning is acting as an agent of slow disclosure, ending, as it does, on the intimate scene of kissing rather than on the still-open possibility of the onlooker watching. The latter would have radically changed the character of our viewing; thus, it becomes apparent that

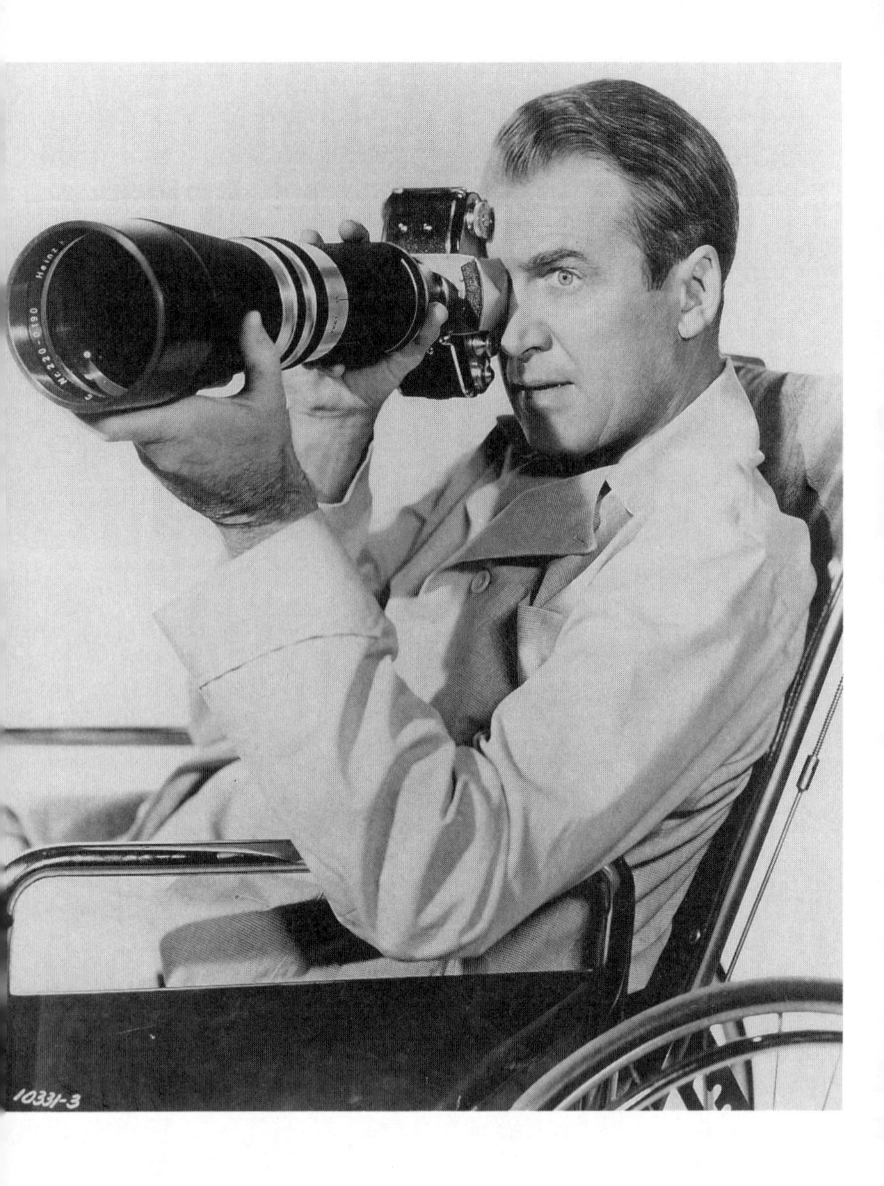
Nr 220-0190
Heinz
10331-3

reality in cinema is not devoid of ambiguity, since a disclosure (at the end of a pan) can color the modality of what was seen before.

The next shot (no. 259), a closer and higher angle of the kissing, shows that Jefferies would rather talk: between kisses he reviews to her the details of the salesman's doings. He is by now totally absorbed in the alleged murder mystery. Lisa eventually gets annoyed with him. Jefferies, still on his subject: "There must be something wrong... What do you think?" She frees herself from his embrace, and retorts: "There must be something wrong with me!" (a rather long duration shot, 31 sec.) She is upset, sits down on the couch by the window, starts smoking. A 13-shot separation follows. Jefferies still talks about the salesman; he looks: a view of the dancer in her bed reading. Jefferies to Lisa: "Just how would you start to cut up a human body?" Lisa lifts herself and says, "Jeff, I'll be honest with you, you begin to scare me!" He hardly hears her. He keeps looking; she too. They see Thorwald entering his apartment holding a heavy rope. He passes to the bedroom, the venetian blinds are down. Jefferies grabs his binoculars. Through the shades he sees the silhouette of the salesman moving from room to room. Shot no. 277 resolves the separation as Lisa comes around, turns Jefferies' wheelchair away from the window and forcefully takes the binoculars out of his hands: "The way you look into people's windows is sick!" He defends himself, pointing to the fate of the salesman's wife.

On the face of it, we are approaching a climax. The whole raison d'être of Jefferies' window gazing is at stake. The verbal exchange lasts 43 sec. The next shot is of about the same duration (46 sec.), a rhythmical twin. Lisa and Jefferies are in profile facing each other. She tries to explain that the wife of the salesman might be peacefully sleeping. She prevents him from returning to his viewing, saying, "There is nothing to see." Lisa, crouching by his knees, tries to explain how irresponsible his hypothesis is. Yet, it takes only six more shots, one minute of screen time, to turn the whole dispute upside down, topsy-turvy!

In shot no. 284 they both notice something across, something riveting; Lisa gets up dramatically (the camera follows), Jefferies moves closer to the window, picks up his field glasses; she rejoins him in the frame; silence . . . they look, we still don't know what they see. Cut to the salesman's bedroom window, whose shade is up by now. A big trunk stands upright on the floor, the thick rope all around it. Thorwald wipes his forehead. The 8-plus sec. of looking and the 6 sec. of the above tableau with the trunk must have affected Lisa sufficiently to sustain and thereby validate a camera movement to her face. In the resulting low close-up she looks transfigured, as she whispers in measured tones: "Let's start from the beginning Jeff... tell me... everything you saw... and... what it... means" (12 sec.). Fade-out.

The suddenness of this fade-out (an intrusive closing into dark) is partially responsible for the success as well as for the credibility of Lisa's unexpected turnabout. The viewers are now forced to complete the scene in their own imagination, play it out, so to speak, with the sinister conclusion that the ominous trunk, *perhaps,* contains the body of Mrs. Thorwald.

The next scenes are brisk as well (shot nos. 287-290). After the fade-in we see a close-up of a hand on a black receiver (3 sec.), then a close-up of Jefferies's face, waiting (3 sec.), followed by a shot of the salesman's three windows in the dark (except for a flashlight) (2 sec.). Finally the phone rings, a close-up of Jefferies answering, Lisa is heard on the other end of the line: she informs him that the salesman's name is Lars Thorwald and gives him the exact address. Jefferies is pleased, tells her to go home and get some sleep. Cut back to the

three windows of Thorwald: in the dark, a single cigarette gleams inside the dining room (6 sec.). Fade-out.

A whirl of happenings has been compressed by the film's deletions (the planning of Lisa's reconnaissance) and its fast clip, providing a fascinating illustration of how cinema language, by a combination of deletions, rhythmic crescendo and a proper fragmentation, can whisk away the need for realistic justification or even for Aristotelian logic (or causality). Hitchcock had successfully used this strategy in *Notorious* (1946) and from then on in most of his films. I should point out, however, that this strategy depends also on the ability of the filmmaker to snip the outgoing scene at the right spot.

The next scene starts with a fade-in, this time after a longer deletion: it is the next day, in the morning. The scene is a release, predictably so, after the outgoing triggers. In addition, it is of longer duration (1 min., 10 sec.) and without cuts. The nurse is preparing breakfast, Jefferies is on the phone with a friend, a New York City detective, whom he asks for help in his investigation. The nurse, as usual, is the provider of comic relief, now peppered with gruesome overtones, like wondering how the salesman cut up his wife, or if the trunk will soon start leaking—all while Jefferies tries to eat his breakfast. The community across is not forgotten. Jefferies watches the dancer as she hangs out some intimate garments on the clothesline. The shade is up at the newlyweds' flat, where the groom puts his head out for air, followed by his wife who is heard calling him back. Jefferies is amused—still, he has to keep watch on Thorwald.

The nurse calls Jefferies to look: two parcel-post men come into Thorwald's apartment to pick up the trunk. The nurse is sent out to check the registration and the name of the trucking company. Jefferies becomes animated: he looks through his field glasses, the trunk is gone. Thorwald, by now in his chair, dials his phone. Jefferies moves his gaze to the alleyway; the nurse comes into view, gesticulating that she missed the truck. Jefferies is visibly disappointed. Fade-out. Again a short deletion—Fade-in later in the day. Shot no. 313 is the first long shot of Jefferies' room looking from the back toward his windows and farther to the windows across. We see, almost in silhouette, two men with their backs to the camera looking out: one is

Jefferies in his chair and, as we shall find out soon, the one standing is the detective friend. This long shot is important for it advances the notion of a fourth wall (in the film), a singular idea of Hitchcock's of far-reaching significance. We shall see the real fourth wall at the end of the film. Yet the former shot and the latter one will be complementary and supportive to each other, a subject that will be elaborated on later in the book.

A reverse shot (incidentally, crossing the axis of view) reveals a frontal view of the detective (Wendel Corey). From the start he will take the role of the devil's advocate: pessimistic about Jefferies' revelations, he argues now and will continue almost to the end of the film that the alleged murder did not occur. At the present time he promises, nevertheless, to "do my own poking around." This scene, as well as the upcoming ones with the detective, is structured, like most dialogue scenes, with a few over-the shoulder shots and many separation shots. (Note that Hitchcock never uses the classical manner of master shot with occasional close-ups and back to the master shot.) Jefferies, as always, is the stable image while the detective moves around the room making the single shots of the separations technically more complex, and dramatically more exciting. Hitchcock became a specialist in the above technique and used this kind of choreography in his later works such as *Frenzy* and *Family Plot*.

After the detective has left the apartment Jefferies, renewing his vigil, sees Thorwald down in the garden pushing the little dog, who had been sniffing the roses, out of the way. Jefferies then sees the detective loitering at the alleyway, also sniffing, in his way. Fade-out.

Again a short deletion, later in the day. We find the detective and Jefferies, drink in hand, going over the situation. So far the detective has found nothing to indicate crime. There is no case that he can see. The dialogue is snappy and sharp (see shot nos. 334 to 364 in Chapter 4). Jefferies defends his position with energy and passion, the detective is cool and professional. A brief relief is afforded by both looking across at the dancer doing her routine. The detective smiles. Jefferies digs in. A 38-shot separation ensues (as mentioned before). The upshot is that there is no evidence. Jefferies begs for a search of

the salesman's apartment: "It must be deep in evidence." The detective retorts with a lecture on judicial procedure, law and the Constitution, the need of search warrants, etc. The doorman and some

tenants have seen, he reports, the salesman leaving with his wife in the morning. Jefferies excitedly retorts, waving his long Chinese scratcher: "Find the trunk"—the detective is about to leave to do some "checking further." At the door he remembers, with a touch of irony: "A postcard from Thorwald's mailbox." He reads: "Arrived. Feeling better. Anna". "You need anything?" Jefferies replies: "No. I need a detective." Left alone, Jefferies lashes out furiously with his scratcher. Eventually he calms down to comical

scratching inside his cast, soothing an actual itch—and reaching nirvana. Fade-out. The scenes with the detective slow down the film—a contrast to the soon-to-start perking up of dramatic bloodstream.

The next fade-in brings us back, later in the evening, to the "detective story." The deletion is short while the scene, unlike the four previous ones, is long, almost 22 min. in duration. There is a fair amount of dialogue, yet the community in the courtyard is not abandoned: the entire scene is bracketed by a new chapter in the subplot of Miss Lonelyhearts. In the process we also visit the little dog, the dancer, the composer, the newlyweds and, of course, the prime target, Mr. Thorwald. In this scene we reach a low point vis-à-vis solving the alleged murder. The detective friend repeatedly dismisses

the meager evidence. In the community, Miss Lonelyhearts is becoming desperate; her expedition to "checher l'homme" ends tearfully. Jeff and Lisa are getting along; they have found a common cause to pursue. The composer has finished his musical score and entertains a crowd of Village intellectuals in his studio. The dancer dances away. The newlyweds continue behind closed doors. And Mr. Thorwald attends to his mystery scheme.

On the formal side, the scene starts with an intriguing slow disclosure: a close-up of a hand reaching for a sandwich. The camera follows it to Jefferies' face as he starts eating and, of course, looking out. He sees the little dog coming down in the above mentioned basket to the garden; the camera pans to the window of Miss Lonelyhearts (this is the first bracket). She is in the process of completing her makeup. Thanks to the telephoto lens we have a new view of her, a much-needed, more intimate look at her exalted pantomime, as she corrects her lipstick, puts on her tiny hat, downs a drink and, on the way to the door, fetches another one; the camera pans with her as she excitedly walks out. This closer look frees us for a while from the framing of the windows and makes it more like a full-fledged silent movie, with the needed variety of shot sizes. The above shot (no. 377) lasts 44 sec. without any cuts. Then we return to Jefferies watching through his telephoto. He sees Miss Lonelyhearts now in the alleyway; reaching the street, she hesitates at a lamppost, then moves across to a bar-restaurant, still in the line of Jefferies' view; she enters and takes a seat before a big window. Suddenly, Hitchcock executes an almost magical transition from this parallel action (Miss Lonelyhearts' story) to the one that is in the center of our (and Jefferies') attention: just as she is about to order a drink, we see outside the restaurant, on the street, the suspected murderer, Thorwald, entering the frame, evidently on his way home. He obliterates our view of Miss Lonelyhearts; then, when he is about to step down to cross the street, a speeding taxi swishes by, almost hitting him; he steps back, startled, then proceeds homeward (30 sec.). The astonishing abruptness of this transition from Lonelyhearts to Thorwald, a cinematic turn of phrase worth remembering, shifts the

action instantly from a subplot to the main theme, in a uniquely cinematic way. (Almost 20 years later, in his last film, *Family Plot,* Hitchcock executes a similar transition from one action to another in a more complex and spectacular way.) It would have been much simpler to execute the transition by a fade-out—yet, the elegance of the language would contract and the play of fate, the hint of an intimate connection of things, would be curtailed.

Jefferies, animated by Thorwald's return, wheels into the shadows, in the back of his room, and watches. He sees Thorwald in the bedroom going over his wife's jewelry while talking on the phone. Attracted by loud music, Jefferies looks up to the composer's studio packed with guests; new ones are still coming in, a party is on. Back to Thorwald who walks to the next room (shot no. 395) and puts away his wife's empty purse. In the next shot we see Jefferies in a wider frame; his door opens and Lisa, displaying a new attaché case, comes in. This sandwiching-in of the composer's party between Thorwald's goings-on is a significant cinematic move (not only a narrative strategy), and has several functions: it slows down the

Thorwald story, is a precursor to Lisa's arrival (later in the scene she'll refer to the music of the composer) and is a release from the intensity of Jefferies' investigation. It also keeps us in touch with the community, since we had left Miss Lonelyhearts for a while. Note that with Lisa's arrival and, to come, the detective's, the drama enters the typical "second act" despondency: a "down" before the upbeat of the following section.

Lisa's entry is elegant and symmetrical to her arrival the day before, notably the way she again puts on the lights one after another.

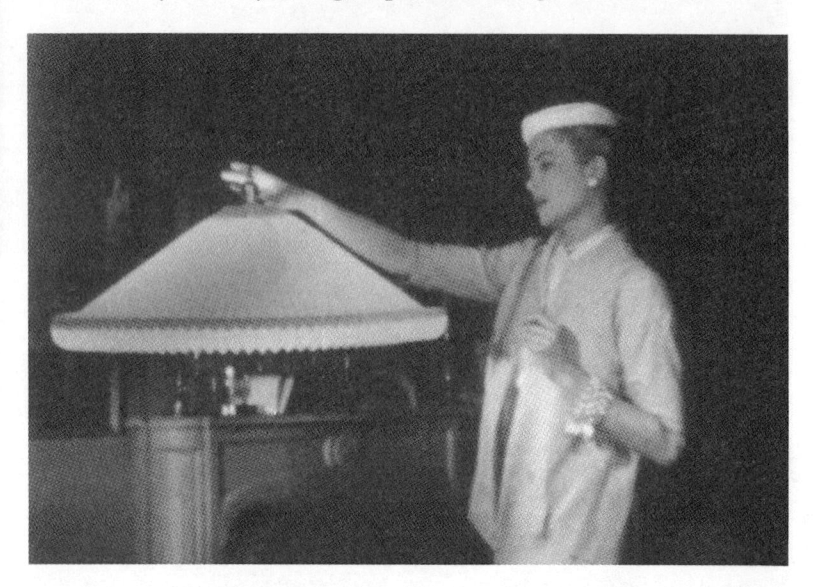

She is briefed by Jefferies on the latest events, especially Thorwald's handling of the jewelry, makeup kit and, most uncommonly, her wedding ring. If the latter can be found in Thorwald's possession it would, in her view, prove beyond any doubt that the worst scenario has taken place. This long duration dialogue shot (no. 404) starts with a crafty separation as Lisa moves around the room, then in and out of a two-shot while she passionately presents her hypothesis: the woman whom witnesses saw leaving with Mr. Thorwald could not have been Mrs. Thorwald! Jefferies eagerly concurs: "I'm with you, I'm with you." The shot lasts 1 min., 30 sec..

In the meantime, as often happens in the detective genre, the victim in question acquires a misty verisimilitude, almost dehumanized; the solving of the crime attains preeminence. Here, besides, we are witnessing a resurgence of Lisa and Jeff's love affair. She sits in his

lap, they kiss, talk intimately; she wants to stay the night, but he has only one bed, so he'll have to sleep on the couch. She shows him her

attaché case, which doubles for a valise with nightgown, slippers, etc.—she is proud to be in his league and to voyage lightly. She then hears music from outside; the camera moves in to a medium close-up of her. He listens and looks outside. A long shot (no. 412) of the composer's studio crowded with guests is in symmetry to its previous appearance. Lisa decides to stay overnight, disregarding Jefferies' worries about the impropriety (remember Hollywood's self-censorship); she leaves the frame to fetch coffee and brandy for both of them. Again the community is woven in, this time the newlyweds. Their shade goes up, the husband leans out for air; the wife is heard calling him back.

As Jefferies watches, his detective friend comes in with news. A vivid fragmentation ensues with brief single and over-the-shoulder shots (2 to 4 sec. each). The detective is introduced to Lisa. He is Jefferies' war buddy from the Air Force. A thinly veiled occasionally amusing jealousy thread about Lisa is introduced between the two men. The pace slows down, culminating in a three shot (all of them in the frame). They talk about the alleged murder, and finally the camera dramatically moves in, into a close-up of the detective, who declares: "Mr. Thorwald is no more a murderer than I am" (shot no. 441, 64 sec.). An eight-shot separation follows between Lisa and Jefferies in one frame and the detective in the other. The rhythm quickens. They press for answers; he has them: everything has been checked out, the trunk, the rail ticket, the witnesses.The case collapses in front of them. They drink the brandy, and they try to make conversation. The detective's eyeing of the attaché case with Lisa's provocative nightgown in it adds a dash of humor to this humorless gathering. A 10-shot separation follows. The social part of the evening does not gel. The detective leaves with the ironic exit line: "Oh, if you need further help, follow the yellow pages in your telephone directory."

Lisa and Jefferies look dejected, almost vacuous. They look out. The party at the composer's is still going strong. Jefferies is scanning the windows across. The dancer is exercising her legs while in bed. Lisa turns his attention to Miss Lonelyhearts, who has just entered the corridor, returning with a real date. The onlookers wonder.

Lonelyhearts serves wine in the dining room, but the man grabs for a kiss. Jefferies shows disapproval. Miss Lonelyhearts breaks away from the impetuous lover to lower the venetian blinds, but we can still see through them. The visitor again seizes her, she struggles and then strikes him on the face. The onlookers, in a frontal two shot, are visibly embarrassed. The "date," upset, starts backing up toward the door and leaves. Miss Lonelyhearts goes back to the table (the camera follows) and collapses, crying (shot no. 479, 26 sec.). Our onlookers, still in the same two shot (no. 480), are depressed; Hitchcock, to emphasize the low ebb, cuts from the familiar two shot of our pair directly to a reverse shot of them, thus crossing the axis of view (and inverting their screen positions). This "super-cut," "crossing the axis," generates energy (albeit subliminally).

Then Lisa moves out of the frame; the camera follows. We hear Jefferies, off screen, expressing ethical compunctions about "watching other people with long lenses." Jefferies in a medium close-up (in profile) continues: "You suppose it is ethical even if he did not commit a crime?" Lisa replies, without turning: "I'm not much on rear-window ethics." In the next shot, which is of longer duration, Lisa, with the camera following her movements around the room, tries to cheer up: "After all, we should be glad the woman was not killed. Instead, we sulk!" She kisses him, lowers their bamboo blinds, in cross symmetry to the opening shot of the film, then goes toward the bathroom to change. Before entering, Lisa asks: "Did the detective solve the case?" Jefferies: "No, Lisa, I don't think he did." Fade-out. This scene lasts almost 20 min.

The fade-in brings us back to Jefferies' room, shortly after. The upcoming and concluding part of the film takes off in a rush, with a predictable sense of an ending: the catharsis-generating event, the death of the little dog—the "deus ex machina" of this drama—takes place in the first shot (no. 489) of the new scene, during the first 22 sec., with a reverberating answer to the question put by Lisa at the end of the outgoing scene ("Did the detective solve the case?").

At first, Lisa executes a humorous, yet exultant, re-entry from the bathroom in her dazzling white nightgown. She floats through the

room as she did on her arrival. Suddenly, we hear a nerve-wracking shriek emanating from the courtyard. Lisa quickly rolls up the blinds. We see her and Jefferies, from behind, watching the dog's owner weeping on the fire escape; the little dog is lying dead downstairs on the concrete. The entire community around the courtyard comes out to sympathize; every window is opened. We see the crowd at the composer's party, the newlyweds, the upstairs-dwellers on the fire escape. A major commotion is compressed into 27 brief shots (1 to 2 sec. in length). The occurrence is ripe in meaning to Jefferies and Lisa. The dog's owner accuses her neighbors: "One of you is the guilty killer." The whole episode, in cinematic terms, is once more like a silent film, charmingly archaic in style, perfectly blended, however, into the fabric.

Lisa and Jefferies bracket the scene at the beginning and the end, and are seen only once in the middle (shot no. 513, 2 sec.), thus legitimizing, discreetly perhaps, their onlooker status. For the first time the protagonists of the subplots (except Thorwald) come out into the open, outside their restricting "screen-windows," and are

seen in close-ups without the help of binoculars or long lenses, liberated, in a sense, from the onlooker's vision. Perhaps that freedom is an additional step toward a sense of the ending, when Thorwald will also come forward to confront Jefferies. The upcoming conclusion, then, will break up, in steps, the oddness and the mystique of the "across."

The scene runs fast (2 to 3 sec. per shot); soon the people return to their abodes and, finally,we come back to Lisa and Jefferies, who, after contemplating the situation, makes the most apt comment: "Look. The only person who did not come out. . . ." Cut to Thorwald's window. It is dark—only the faint glow of a cigarette can be seen behind the blinds. Back to the medium close-up of Jefferies and Lisa; they opine that the dog was killed "because he knew too much." Then another, closing, shot of Thorwald's dark window with the cigarette still burning (no. 527, 10 sec.); fade-out.

Fade-in, longer deletion, next morning, same location. In a long shot (no. 528) we see, this time, three onlookers, their backs to the camera, the windows across also in view. Lisa and the nurse stand on the right, Jefferies in his chair is on the left. This camera position is significant since it again ploddingly accomodates the notion of a fourth wall, i.e. that Jefferies is indeed also across, from the point of view of the people in the windows (eventually, at the end of the film, this will be accomplished with fervor.)

The next shot (no. 529) is a reverse of the above, again crossing the axis, again a Hitchcockian super-cut for emphasis. Jefferies is now on the right; Lisa and the nurse face the camera, and look across. Thorwald is seen through his bathroom window washing down the wall above the tub. The nurse, with her morbid-comic remark, "The blood must have splattered on the wall," unnerves Lisa. The plot gets more intense. To slow it down Hitchcock introduces a rather lengthy, yet partially inconclusive, search through Jefferies' set of photo slides of the garden that, upon viewing, show changes in the position of the flowers and, thus, leads them to think that Thorwald might have buried his wife's body in there—a clue as to why the dog was killed (shot nos. 535 to 542, almost 2 min. long in duration). Finally, a quick decision: Jefferies wheels himself around and asks for

a piece of paper. In a high camera angle (shot no. 544) he starts scribbling a note—the camera moves in to a close-up—that reads: "What have you done with her?" He folds it and starts addressing an

envelope to Lars Thorwald. Before he finishes, Hitchcock employs his magic: after a lengthy and almost insipid release with the photo slides comes an energetic spin of the plot, and then an incision of a fade-out before the ending of the action.

Fade-in (shot no. 545). A brief deletion. Once more a long shot with the onlookers, their backs to the camera (as in no. 528), Jeff with long lens on the ready. Cut to the alleyway; Lisa, with the letter in hand, waves to Jeff and leaves the frame.

The final, upcoming, chapter of the film is filled with action and genuinely rank suspense. The looking inverses itself: instead of peeping

"there," where before endured a dim sensation of daydream, fantasy or even nightmare, the reality now sets in. Lisa finds herself in the lion's den, in Thorwald's apartment; eventually the lion himself gradually comes in contact with the peeper. At the end, he even intrudes on Jefferies' premises, ready to kill. The very subject of Lisa and Jefferies' search—the drama that gave them a common goal—gave a lift to their relationship and becomes their drama, with both Lisa and Jeff in great danger.

Hitchcock's suspense-making mastery is quite evident: after Lisa leaves the frame on her way to deliver the letter, the film cuts back to the two shot of the nurse and Jefferies (backs to the camera) looking, with the help of the lens and binoculars; next, a reverse shot (again, crossing the axis) of the two. Jeff takes the lens down, since it will not be needed. The next shot (no. 549) will contain a parallel action of Lisa in Thorwald's corridor putting the letter under his door, Thorwald in his apartment noticing it and walking over to check. The setup calls for several windows in the frame, i.e. a wide long shot (which the long lens would have eliminated). The shot lasts 24 sec. but is followed by a series of brief ones, cutting back and forth between Thorwald and the onlooking Jefferies (who brings up the long lens again). The chain of shots here is characteristic of the language, showing how the onlooker "directs" the content by using or not using the long lens:

Shot no. 547: Two shot from the back; Jefferies looks through the lens (3 sec.).

Shot no. 548: Reverse shot—*frontal crossing-the-axis*—Jefferies puts the lens away, thus permitting for a wider shot to follow (3 sec.).

Shot no. 549: Long shot of all of Thorwald's windows. Parallel action starts: Thorwald in the bedroom smokes a cigar (screen right); at the same time Lisa, in the corridor, tiptoes to Thorwald's door (screen left) and slips the envelope under it; she hurriedly retreats. Thorwald, alerted by the noise, walks over, passing three windows, and picks up the letter from the floor. Lisa has already left (24 sec.).

Shot no. 550: Cut back to the two shot of the nurse and Jefferies who again looks through the lens (2 sec.).

Shot no. 551: Cut to a medium close-up of Thorwald as he opens the envelope and starts reading (6 sec.).

Until now Jefferies, by changing the direction of his gaze, had given us a hint of what to expect in the next shot; now, we can judge by the presence or absence of the lens (or binoculars) what will be the shape of the next image. Suspense is actively created with the help of the onlookers as they respond to what they see during the brief fragmented shots, in this case when Lisa is in danger (ever since she physically traversed the barrier of the "acrossness" to the other side of the courtyard). Previously, the onlookers' reactions were mostly relaxed and pacific; by now, they are not outsiders anymore—they are engaged. Watching them clues us on how to react, like here, when the nurse clutches Jefferies as Thorwald runs down the corridor after Lisa, searching for her on the fire escape. We are relieved when Lisa hides successfully downstairs, prodding the nurse to mutter, appropriately: "Thank heaven that's over," as she turns to the kitchen for a drink of whiskey.

The community is not forgotten in the midst of all the excitement. The nurse looks through the long lens and sees Miss Lonelyhearts handling a bottle of red pills, getting water. She voices concern (shot no. 566).

In the meantime, Lisa returns to Jefferies' apartment, asking eagerly: "What was his reaction when he read the note?" Jefferies looks at her admiringly—she is his hero; this brief, 4 sec. shot (no. 571) of Jefferies in close-up is a significant crowning in a new phase of their relationship.

They keep watching Thorwald; he takes his wife's handbag and steps into the space behind the wall (between windows), then comes out and throws the handbag into his valise. Lisa and Jefferies discusss the new situation. The main focus is on the wedding ring—is it there? During this long-duration three shot (1 min., 30 sec.) they go over several scenarios. For one, Lisa wants to go into the garden to dig for possible remains, but Jefferies objects. Lisa then insists the wedding ring would provide the needed proof, as far as she is concerned. Jeff has an idea to phone Thorwald directly and lure him out of his apartment. One more shot (no. 575) of the dejected Miss

Lonelyhearts, who sits. Jefferies dials the number; they watch Thorwald, who hears the ring, walks to the phone, stalls. Jefferies, in close-up with receiver in hand, encourages his adversary to pick up the phone (across): "Go ahead, pick it up" (shot no. 578, 2 sec.). Several shots are repeated of Jefferies and then Thorwald, who still hesitates then finally picks it up. Jefferies: "Did you get my note?" Thorwald is frozen. Jefferies drives harder: "Did you get it?" Finally, the electronic contact between them is accomplished. Five more shots of short duration are used for the actual negotiation where Jefferies proposes a meeting between them in the Albert Hotel: "Something about your wife. . . . "

The uncanny scheme Jefferies has devised to get Thorwald out of his apartment is working. The visual scheme displaying this fascinating duel of nerves is cast in a simple mosaic of shots, constant in picture size though variable in rhythm: Jefferies in medium close-ups, Thorwald in intriguing long shots, some containing several windows as well as Thorwald's small, wretched figure trapped, depicting his sorry state solely in body language. A medium two shot of Lisa and the nurse is three times intercut, as they listen to Jefferies' side of the phone conversation. Finally, Thorwald mumbles: "I don't know what you mean." Jefferies threatens to call the police; Thorwald is silent. Jefferies says, mendaciously: "I'm in the Albert Hotel now. I'll be looking for you." Thorwald (in the same long shot) weakens; he hangs up the receiver, then puts on his straw hat and bolts over toward the door, passing from window to window into the corridor. The repeated long shots of Thorwald pay off magnificently in dramatic impact when juxtaposed against the medium close-up of Jefferies, the onlooker-aggressor. Simple-minded filmmaking would have led to the opposite conclusion. The prevailing logic is in favor of the effectiveness of the close-up as the ultimate punch line of a cinematic phrase. In the hands of a master, the long shot, in the proper chain of shots, can have an imprint stronger than an explicit close-up.

The above scene unquestionably begins the change in both narrative and film language from Jefferies' passive onlooking to his personal interaction. The onlooker gives up his Peeping Tom isolation, the loneliness of the voyeur; he has made the first active contact, one-sided so far, but nevertheless a penetration to the "other side." The full-scale eye contact between both sides is to come soon, yet there will be more intense silent-film episodes before all parties eventually meet physically. The viewer of the film now will start seeing the drama more objectively. In other words, the total domination of what is seen will slowly start escaping from the monopoly of Jefferies' choices.

In the meantime, with Thorwald out of the way, Lisa and the nurse leave the room to dig in the garden for any remains of Mrs.

Thorwald. Jefferies promises to keep guard; he picks up the camera and starts looking (shot no. 600). He sees, with his telephoto, Thorwald passing through the alleyway on the way to the street. Jefferies wheels around his room preparing flash equipment, in case he has to signal the women of Thorwald's return (shot no. 602, 27 sec.). Then, we see the two women crossing the garden via the stairs, reminding us of the crossing of the black cat from the beginning of the film. The next 11 shots feature the nurse and Lisa digging with Jefferies on the watch, nervously looking on, occasionally exchanging gestures with Lisa; he also tries, so far unsuccessfully, to phone the detective. Twelve shots later we visit briefly a jam session in the composer's studio (shot no. 615, 3 sec.). More digging follows and again, so as not to abandon the community, a long shot of Miss Lonelyhearts by her window, writing, presumably a suicide note; she hears the music, gets up as if inspired (shot no. 619, 7 sec.). Jefferies, more nervous as the time passes, picks up his telephoto lens, looks at the alleyway, then pans to the nurse digging; she gestures to him that nothing is found. Jefferies puts away the long lens, disappointed and worried (5 sec.).

In the next shot (no. 623) *we* see Lisa running to the fire escape across and starting to climb, her elegant Parisian skirt flowing as she tries to reach Thorwald's window. It is important to note that we see Lisa's bold action on our own, not at Jefferies' direction; he might or might not have even seen it as yet. The pictorial information appears first to us, the viewers, characteristically, as a sign of liberation from Jefferies' control of the viewing. Only next comes the expected shot of Jefferies, faintly crying out: "Lisa, what are you doing?" (shot no. 624, 3 sec.). Lisa keeps climbing up. Cut back to the same medium close-up of Jefferies, in a state of desperation (2 sec.). In the meantime, Lisa, in long shot, has reached Thorwald's window; it won't open. Repeat of Jefferies' close-up; he almost shouts out: "Don't!" (2 sec.). Lisa climbs over a balcony, and leaps up and into the murderer's lair through the open dining room window (shot no. 629, 17 sec.). Cut back to the same shot of Jefferies, who tosses his head against the edge of his window frame in total resignation (2 sec.) Then follow several shots of Lisa running around Thorwald's

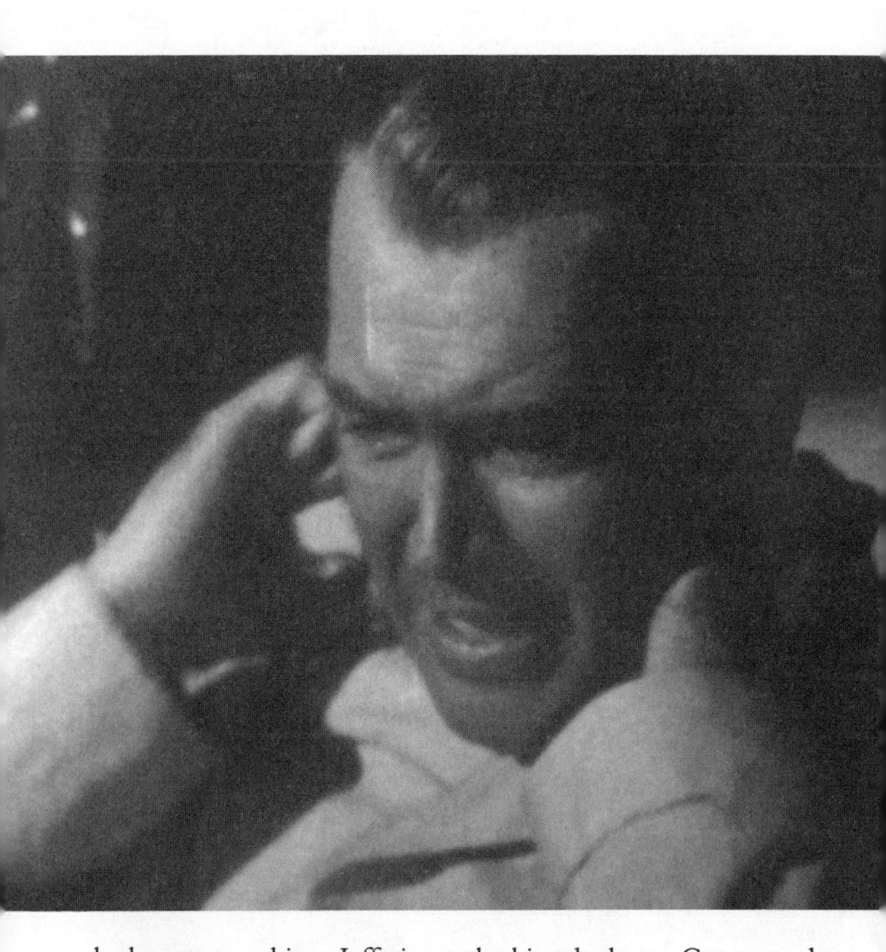

bedroom, searching. Jefferies grabs his telephoto. Cut to a close medium shot of Lisa (via the telephoto) searching the valise. She gestures to Jefferies. Back to the same medium close-up of Jefferies as he takes away the lens and furiously shouts: "Get out of there!" He again nervously checks the alleyway for Thorwald's return. Cut to a long shot of Lisa searching a chest of drawers. The next shot abandons the constant close-up of Jefferies; instead we see him in medium long shot as he turns in his wheelchair to the door. The nurse enters; she insists he call the police (7 sec.).

The above switch in Jefferies' picture size signals the upcoming increase in tension, for which Hitchcock needs a full scale of varied framings. Lisa is still searching the drawers (2 sec.). Then a deliberate interruption, back to Miss Lonelyhearts. In long shot, we see her behind her drawn blinds handling the bottle of pills. The nurse implores Jefferies to call the police. Back to Miss Lonelyhearts still holding the pills (7 sec.). Cut to a 1 sec. shot of Jefferies on the phone. Again we are interrupted by a brief shot of the composer's studio where the group is playing the theme melody that serves as the background sound to the last several shots. Cut to Miss Lonelyhearts getting up; she takes notice of the tune, and leans forward to hear better. Cut to Lisa in a much wider long shot, she stops her search for a moment, evidently also responding to the melody; then she pantomimes to

Jefferies and shows him a necklace. Suddenly we see on the far left, through a small window, the bulky figure of Thorwald gloomily plowing in the corridor towards his door (shot no. 647, 6 sec.). In the next shot, Jefferies, who's still on the phone, and the nurse notice, to their horror, Thorwald's return. Again we, the audience, have seen the event first, before Jefferies. Interestingly enough, Lisa is becoming the vehicle behind our gradual liberation from Jefferies' "viewing across process." The film's audience will start carrying more of the burden of objective seeing—a balance is forming itself as the film approaches closure.

A brief cut to the still unaware Lisa, who suddenly becomes alarmed as she hears someone at the door. (In the wide frame we see her as well as the corridor window with Thorwald opening the door.) Cut to a different framing of Jefferies and the nurse: a tight low close-up of the two faces in three-quarter low profile, intensely dramatic; the

nurse puts her hand on her mouth, mumbling: "Lisa, Lisa." The change of framing also affects Lisa's next shot: she is seen closer, in a medium long shot (in one window only). She runs in panic back to the dining room (the camera follows her), then to the bedroom where she steps out of view in the space between the windows; a reflection in the glass of a half-opened window mirrors Thorwald as he enters the apartment, shutting the door behind him (shot no. 651, 11 sec.).

The above closer shot, covering just one window in Thorwald's apartment, has not been justified by any realistic device (like binoculars), yet it was sneaked in to present more efficiently the byplay between the two sides from each other across: the dramatic close-up of Jefferies and the nurse versus the shot of Thorwald's entry and the entrapment of Lisa.

Cut to Jefferies (in the close two shot), who finally has the police station on the phone: "A man is molesting a woman." (He gives the address, etc.). Cut to the other side: Thorwald walks to his bedroom (camera follows), passing two windows; he looks around, notices something (9 sec.). Next, a brief shot (1 sec.) of the same dramatic three-quarter profile of Jefferies and the nurse frozen in horror. Cut back to Thorwald, who picks up his wife's empty bag, then turns, spotting Lisa (7 sec.). Once more a repeat of the dramatic two shot of the overwhelmed Jefferies and the nurse (1 sec.). Cut back to

Thorwald; the climax reaches its peak as he walks over to the space behind the wall. Lisa emerges as she backs out into the dining room, holding something behind her back (13 sec.). Again, a change of framing: Jefferies is seen in close-up (we see parts of the nurse's figure next to him). The next 17 shots (from no. 656 to no. 673) are structured in the classical alternating "a-b-a-b" rhythm, between the new close-up of Jefferies and the medium long shot of Thorwald's apartment. He grabs Lisa's arm, twisting it as she fends off (the shots last 2 to 5 sec.). James Stewart pantomimes brilliantly his anxiety and helplessness with a whole range of actorial techniques, tenable and unimpeachable in its dramatic effect.

Lisa defends herself as Thorwald keeps pounding, then turns off the light. Jefferies shouts out: "What are we going to do?" Across, the struggle continues in the dark; Jefferies grabs his neck with both hands, and the nurse's voice announces: "Look! The police are coming!" (2 sec.). The sequence takes a turn with changed framing: a wider long shot covering several windows shows the police entering the corridor, stopping at Thorwald's door as the latter reacts to the knocking from the dark dining room. The close-up of Jefferies is replaced by the familiar two shot with the nurse in the same frame. They are overtaken with relief; soon Jefferies picks up his telephoto lens.

Back to the long shot of Thorwald's windows—the police ring the bell again, Thorwald puts on the light. Lisa is getting up from the floor and Thorwald starts moving toward the door (shot no. 673, 10 sec.). Jefferies and the nurse look on. Thorwald is at the door; Lisa straightens herself out; Jefferies lifts his telephoto lens to his eye (2 sec.). Via the long lens we see Thorwald in medium shot (alone, the closest we have seen him so far), opening the door quite

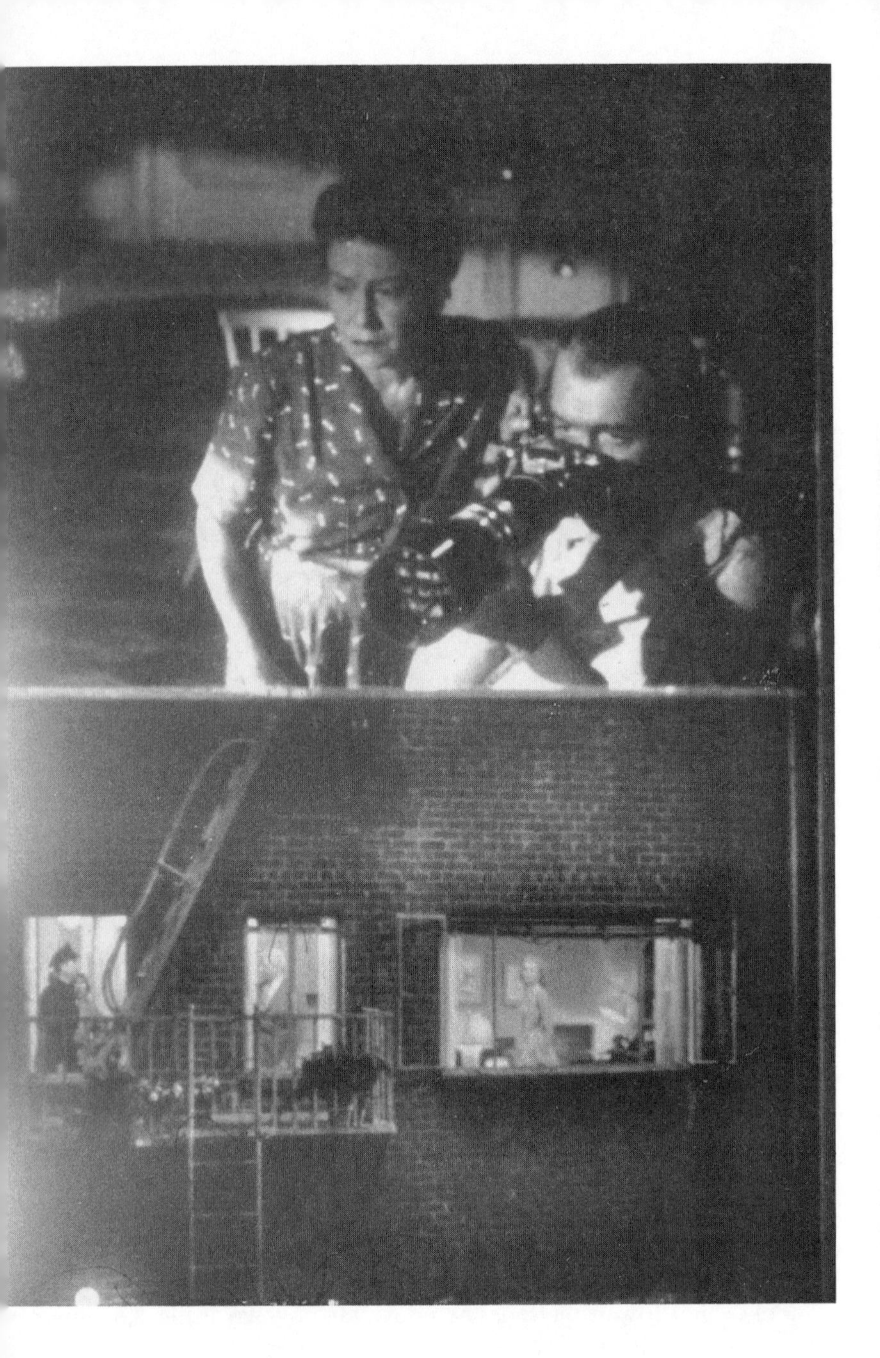

apprehensively, then turning to Lisa (who is out of frame), pointing at her accusingly as to the intruder (10 sec). Back to the two onlookers, Jefferies puts away the lens (2 sec.). Cut to the *wider* long shot of the windows. Thorwald follows the police to the dining room. They approach Lisa, her back to the camera. Thorwald shows the purse to the police. The next five shots go back and forth between the two sides, as Jefferies looks again through his long lens (shot no. 680). Consequently, we see the Thorwald apartment in close shots as he

dickers with the police. Finally, in shot no. 685 we see Lisa's back in close-up; behind her back she is pointing to the wedding ring she has found and put on her finger, knowing that Jefferies is watching, thinking that no one else can see her. The camera pans down to the ring for a better view, then up to Thorwald who stands next to her; facing the camera in close up, he slyly notices her gesticulation, and looks across towards Jefferies' window. He now has a clue, a decisive one, about where his tormentor is located (9 sec.).

Cut to Jefferies, who quickly pulls back his wheelchair from the window and asks the nurse to turn off the lights (5 sec.). Next, we see in a wider long shot the police moving out of Thorwald's apartment, taking Lisa with them (4 sec.). A longer-duration shot follows (35 sec.) providing a release after a long series of triggers; Jefferies is sending the nurse off with money to bail out Lisa from the police station. Cut back to the dark room of Thorwald, who seems to get ready to go out as he looks across. Jefferies gets on the phone; left alone, he starts a hushed, yet frantic, phone conversation with his friend the detective. The camera moves in closer; the detective is still pessimistic about the case. Jefferies, defending his position, also looks at the window across. This long-duration shot, (1 min., 37 sec.), offers a certain precursor of something coming.

After a 3 sec. shot of Thorwald's dark window, cut to a medium close-up of Jefferies. He picks up his ringing receiver sure that his friend is calling. He starts speaking about Thorwald, then realizes it

is not his friend on the line. A dead silence, as the other party clicks down. Jefferies, in terror, looks across. The camera moves in into his close-up (44 sec.).

The next 12 shots are a byplay between Jefferies alone, trapped in his room in his wheelchair, and the impending disaster, represented by the narrow slit of light under his door. Between Jefferies tossing and scrounging for ideas to defend himself this light under the door is intercut three times for 1 to 3 sec. at a time. The shots of Jefferies are longer as he wheels around the room (multiangular camera positions), finally coming upon an idea to use his powerful flash bulbs. The light under the door fatefully goes out, and heavy steps are heard approaching. Jefferies, in a medium shot, is terrified. In shot no. 708 the door finally opens, slowly, and Thorwald moves in, backlit by the corridor light, ominous and bear-like (14 sec.).
Thorwald's entry resolves the expectation of the unknown, and in some sense the suspense of one kind ends and a new and more intense one starts. Most important, the mystique of the "other side,"

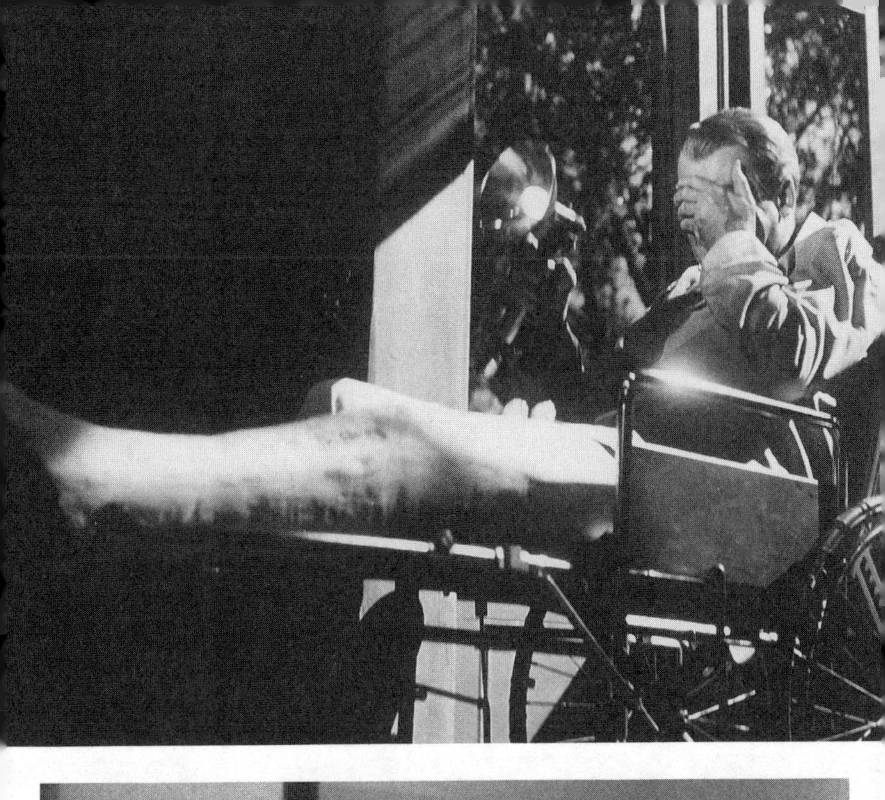

of the "absurd across," is almost eliminated, and a new dimension of dramatics begins as the observed meets the onlooker. The quality of looking suddenly metamorphoses from the not-so-concrete dream-like and safe watching of little movies in the windows across to a real involvement with a desperate murderer in flesh, who suddenly leaves the imaginary silver screen and enters "your house"—such is the viewer's identification with Jefferies.

Thorwald's portentous entry into Jefferies' room commences the most climactic action scene in the film, a model of its kind in cinematic structure. To summarize the narrative: Thorwald barges into the dark room; Jefferies, after a brief panic, starts firing large photographic flashes in order to delay the imminent attack. The effect is horrific, a bright, blue glow followed by a pink-red aftershock repeated four times. Thorwald, blinded at first, lurches forward, striking and pounding Jefferies and pushing him toward the window; he finally succeeds in thrusting him over, but Jefferies somehow manages to hang on to the edge of the sill. The scene contains genuine suspense, even brutality, yet upon thorough examination it is far from the "slice of life" mayhem seen in contemporary films. Rather, it is a mosaic of details, some almost abstract, that only in sum spell the realistic content. The basic elements employed here by Hitchcock are: multiangularity, frequent changes in framing (yet, interestingly enough, with several repetitions) and, most important, a minute yet precise fragmentation that controls the rhythm of the scene.

To start, the rhythmic pulsation is rather slow: each of the 12 long shots after Thorwald's entry is only 2 to 4 sec. long. The beginning of the struggle consists of 17 shots from 1 to 2.5 sec. each, followed by 7 shots (0.5 to 1 sec. each), and by a montage of very brief half-second shots that show eyes, fingers, arms, elbows, legs, etc.. There are several half-second intercuts to the principal members of the courtyard community looking on from across—they become onlookers now. We are not shown what they see, although it is assumed that they look at Jefferies' window. (The assumption is an important plant for the final resolution.)

The newlyweds are the last of the community onlookers, standing at their window as they watch Jefferies' drama. The significant as-

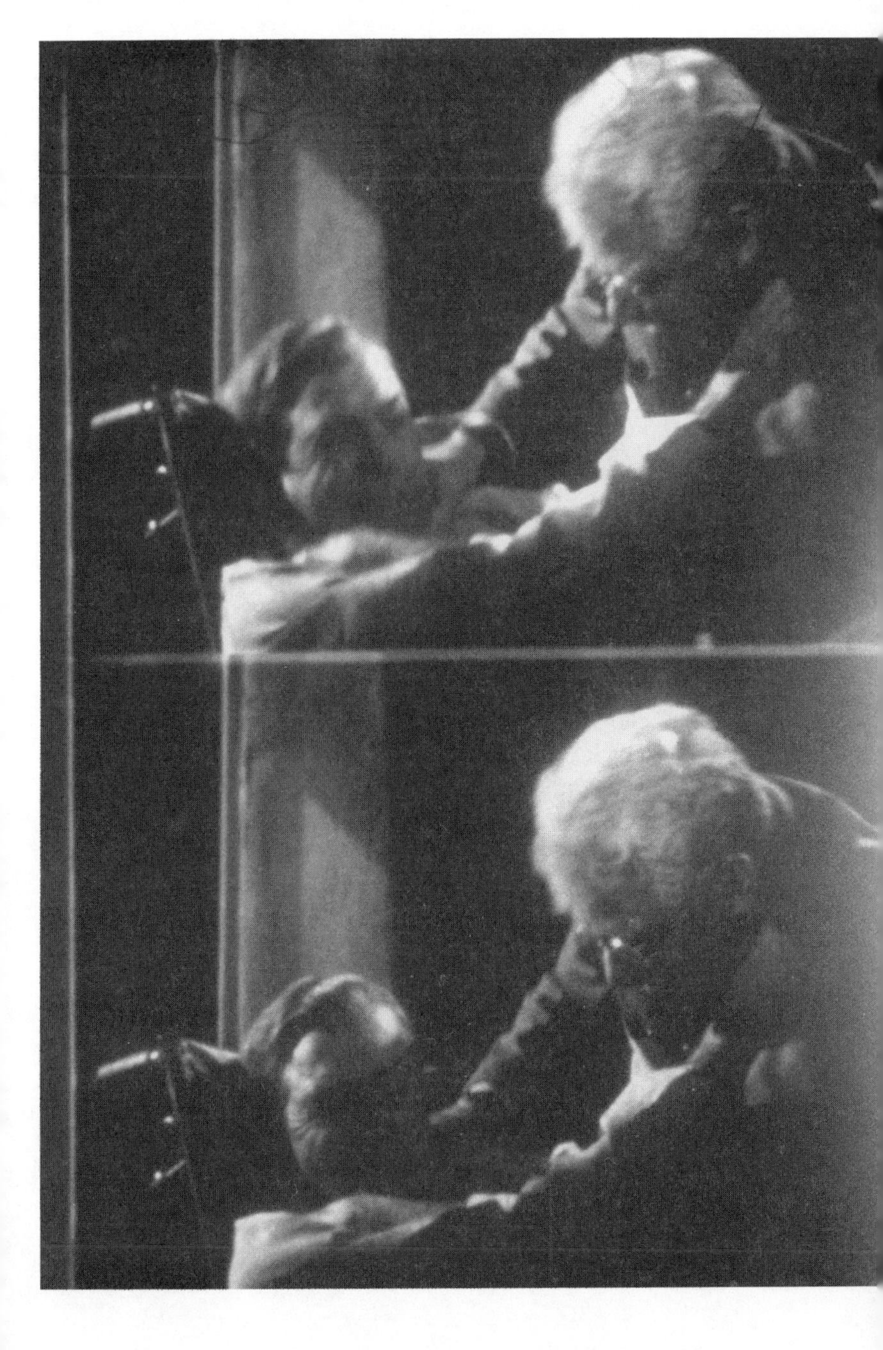

pect here is the length of this shot: at 1.5 sec. it is much longer than the previous shots, thus slowing down the rhythm of the sequence. Consequently the next shot, no. 776, almost stops the rhythmic pulsation, as it lasts 9 sec. and contains a moving camera mode rather than cuts: the camera pans with the police as they rush through the garden, then continues panning up to a long shot of Jefferies dangling down but still hanging on to his second-floor window, his back to the camera. This is the most crucial reverse shot in the film, the cinematic tour de force; for the first time we see the geographically correct other side of the "across," the fourth wall of the film. One reacts not only to the tragic-comic figure of our protagonist but also, subliminally, to the revelation of the "fourth wall." Hitchcock most deliberately delays it to the end of the film. Striving for complexity in this case, through a sudden reverse of the angle of looking, he inverts the situation and folds it upon itself: the original onlooker becomes the target of view, another kind of symmetry, perspicatiously spelled out in cinema language.

The dream is definitely over—what follows is rather routine: the police, in a 1 sec. shot, pull Thorwald away from the window. A brief reverse high shot, from the interior looking out, shows Jefferies letting go and falling down out of frame. A half-second medium

long shot completes Jefferies' fall, almost into the arms of the police below; a triad of brief close-ups finalizes his landing. The quick pace is broken by a panning shot of the detective, then Lisa and the nurse entering the frame to Jefferies' side (8 sec.). The expected close-up

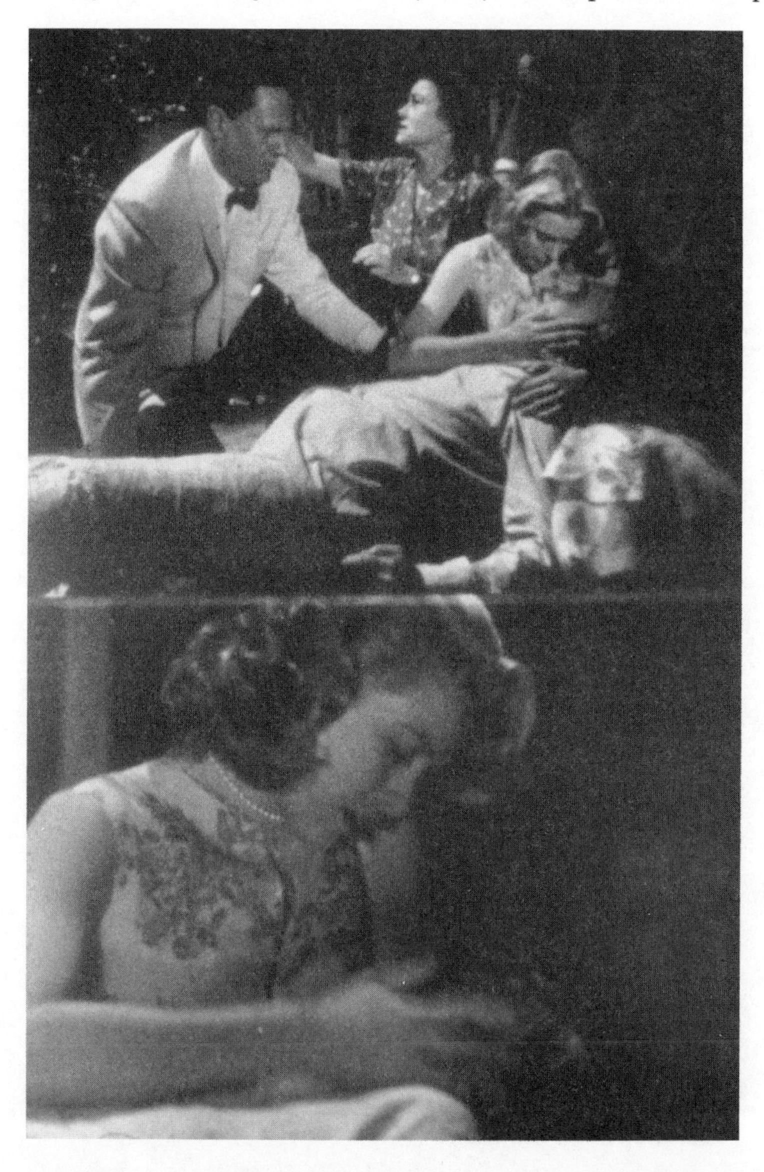

of Jefferies follows, with Lisa next to him. "I'm proud of you," he tells her, then, to the detective (who is out of frame): "Now you'll file for a search warrant?" (9 sec.). Interestingly enough, Jefferies is briefly "abandoned" after the above shot. In the next eight shots we learn that Thorwald has confessed and is going to give the police a macabre tour of the sites where he buried different parts of his wife. A bit of black comedy ends the scene: the nurse, whom we know for her morbid humor, is informed that some part of Mrs. Thorwald that was originally buried in the garden, until the dog sniffed it out, is presently up in the apartment, in a hat box. The detective mischievously asks her: "Do you want to have a look?" Cut to a close-up of the nurse (the first close-up of her in the entire film) who, after a moment of hesitation, answers: "No, I don't want to have any part of it!" A spectacular fade-out. Thus, Hitchcock ends the scene comedically, lightly glossing over its intricateness.

The real finale follows: an entire closing scene lasting 1 min., 42 sec. without cuts, with the camera panning relentlessly over the whole spectrum of windows. A grand symmetry mirrors the opening of the film, except that this time we are familiar with the sites and the people. Fade-in to a thermometer, showing a mild 70°. The camera pans slowly to the composer's studio, where Miss Lonelyhearts listens to a recording of the theme melody and the composer converses

with her in a cordial manner. (We are again in a silent mode—only the music can be heard.) Miss Lonelyhearts is in good spirits. The camera starts panning again to the windows of Thorwald's former apartment, where painters are at work. Next, the camera reaches the fire escape, showing a new dog in the basket ready to be sent downstairs. Then comes to view the window of the dancer who, upon hearing someone at the door, stops her dancing. In comes a short, bespectacled GI in uniform, her husband, ironically; she greets him passionately. The camera passes by the sculptor, who sleeps in her chaise longue, then by the window with the birdcage seen in the beginning of the film. Next, in an upward movement, we pass by the newlywed's little window, where they are breakfasting at the

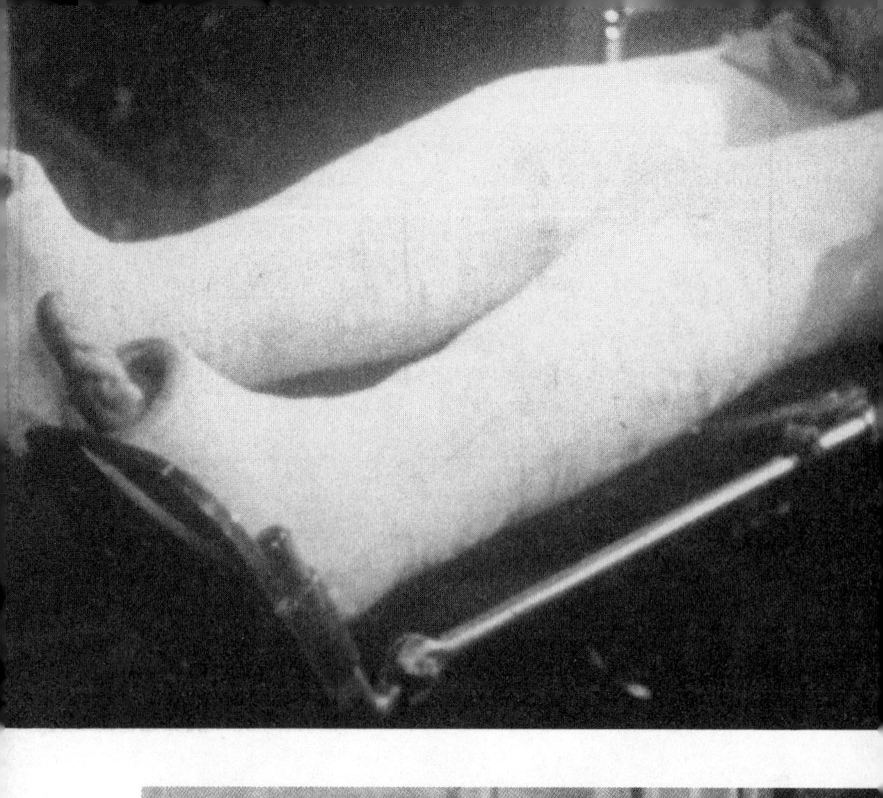

BEYOND THE HIGH

table as the wife serves coffee. Finally, the camera climbs up to Jefferies' windows: in close-up, he sleeps, this time peacefully with a smile on his face. Camera pans down revealing two casts on his legs with two pair of toes clowning at us. The camera keeps panning to a close-up of Lisa reclining on the couch by the window, reading a book on the Himalayas; she checks to see if Jefferies is still sleeping, then picks up *Harper's Bazaar* and leafs through it with relish. The film ends on her image, her victory of sorts. Fade-out. Not only is this scene a grand symmetry, but it is also a total resolution to the problems that clouded the whole community, in the subplots and the main plot, with a light touch of humor and a lingering suspicion of the sinister, underside of everyday life. Thus Hitchcock projected his tale and the flickering silver screen fades; the viewers, dazed by the light, collect their thoughts, reaching into the many niches of meaning, open-ended, to be sure, to various interpretations, just as a classic work would surely bring forth.

4

SHOT BY SHOT (WITH TIMING AND DIALOGUE)

THIS CHAPTER contains, as the title connotes, a description of every shot: framing, action and timing. In short it is a formal and technical scheme of the entire work. The reader not interested in these details need not be concerned with this chapter. It does, however, provide the complete dialogue as heard in the film and the material I refer to by shot number in other chapters.

1. Titles—credits—set with city skyline as backdrop. (1 min., 5 sec.) Bamboo shades go up.

2. Camera dollies out of a window toward the wall and windows across, in long shot. (6 sec.)

3. Cut to high long shot of garden area, a black cat walks up some stairs, camera follows, cat leaves the frame, camera continues up a fire-escape ladder to an upper balcony with two people standing, then pans left to a wall with windows; in one of them, we see a woman brushing her hair. The camera pans down to the ground level, then up again and left, revealing, unexpectedly in close-up, the heavily sweating face of Jimmy Stewart, sleeping. (40 sec.)

4. Cut to a close-up of a wall thermometer showing 93°F; after a three-second hold, camera continues to pan to the left, reaching a medium long shot of a large studio window, behind which we see a baby grand piano and a bed. A man stands lathering his face with a brush; he stops, walks over to the radio, which is blasting commercials, and tunes in some music. (14 sec.)

5. Cut to medium long shot of a fire-escape platform; a man in pajamas sits up from his sleep, then a woman from the other end of the bed sits up (they apparently are sleeping outside); camera starts panning to the left and down closer to the windows—we pass a small window—with a woman still (see shot no. 3) brushing her hair, she walks over to the big window in the adjacent room. Camera pans with her, and we see her back as she puts on a bra, then she turns and dances over to pick up a coffeemaker, doing her chores while exercising. Camera starts again panning to the left, then pans down to the ground level; we see an alleyway with a narrow view to the street, a garbage truck passes, camera continues along the left wall as a woman takes off the cover from a birdcage; eventually, the camera comes upon a medium close-up of the head of James Stewart, still

sleeping (in symmetry with the end of shot no. 3). After a pause, camera pans down along his body to reveal a full cast on his left leg inscribed with his name—L.B. Jefferies—in large letters; camera pulls back to a medium long shot of the wheelchair he is sitting in. The roving camera starts showing a smashed 8x10 view camera, possibly from the accident that caused his fractured leg, then up the wall to several large photos of auto racing, a military explosion, a burning car in a war zone and, finally, to a framed negative transparency of a young woman next to a stack of magazines with the same portrait as the above negative on their cover. *FADE-OUT. So far, this is the longest-duration moving camera shot.* (1 min., 40 sec.)

6. *FADE-IN.* Later the same morning: medium long shot of Jefferies using an electrical shaver. Street noises, the city is awake. Jefferies is on the phone talking to his boss at the magazine. (13 sec.)

7. Cut to medium long shot of the roof terrace; we see two women (partially behind a low wall) throwing over their pajamas, possibly settling down to sunbathe. (12 sec.)

8. Cut to a low medium shot of Jefferies on the phone, yet looking in the direction of the roof. The phone conversation deals mostly with the hope that he shall be liberated shortly from his cast which has been on for six weeks. The talk continues over the next few shots as Jefferies observes the views across from him. (2 sec.)

9. Cut to long shot of a civilian helicopter lowering in for a closer view of the girls on the roof. (6 sec.)

10. Cut back to the same medium shot of Jefferies on the phone: "Next Wednesday I get rid of my cocoon." He looks up to the helicopter with a smile then lowers his gaze. (8 sec.)

11. Cut to medium long shot of the dancer, who continues to dance, combining it with minor chores: She approaches the refrigerator, bends down and wiggles. (9 sec.)

12. Cut to medium close-up of Jefferies still on the phone and looking at what he sees of the dancer with savor. (2.5 sec.)

13. Cut to the same medium shot of the dancer as she keeps wiggling her shapely behind more provocatively while searching for something on the lower shelf of the refrigerator. (2 sec.)

14. Cut back to a low medium close-up of Jefferies looking on at the

dancer with interest, while talking with his boss about his next assignment. (6 sec.)
15. Cut back to the medium shot of the dancer as she turns away from the refrigerator, dancing and eating a stick of celery. (10 sec.)
16. Cut back to the same shot of Jefferies smiling. (3 sec.)
17. Cut back to dancer; her upper part is more prominent. (2 sec.)
18. Cut back to the same shot of Jefferies, still on the phone—small talk about his boredom: "Nothing to do but watch my neighbors," he says with double entendre. He continues looking out. (4 sec.)
19. Cut back to same shot of dancer, who makes herself a sandwich and starts eating while dancing. (10 sec.)
20. Cut back to the same shot of Jefferies talking on the phone; he changes the direction of his gaze down. (3 sec.)
21. Cut to a high medium long shot of the ground-floor apartment of the sculptress, whom we see inside busy with something. She reacts to a noise outside by turning her face. (5 sec.)
22. Cut back to the same shot of Jefferies on the phone; he again changes his gaze. (2 sec.)
23. Cut to a medium long shot of the musician's studio. He is at the piano, and turns his face reacting to a noise, then turns back to his notes, correcting with a pencil. (7 sec.)
24. Cut back to Jefferies, who implores by phone: "You have to get me out of here, or else I'll get married and all will. . . ." (5 sec.)
25. Cut back to the same shot of the musician, who plays a tune, then gets up, annoyed by some noise. Jefferies: "Six weeks—sitting in a two-room apartment with nothing to do but look out the window at the neighbors." (5 sec.)
26. Cut back to the same shot of Jefferies; again he changes his gaze. (2 sec.)
27. Cut to the three windows of the traveling salesman Mr. Thorwald (Raymond Burr) in a wide long shot. We see him walking in the corridor to his door, entering the apartment, walking to the middle window. He takes off his jacket; camera pans with him as he proceeds to the next room where a woman (his wife wearing a negligée) is sitting. (On the soundtrack, we hear Jefferies continuing his conversation: "If I'm gonna get married I won't be able to go anyplace

anymore"; the voice of his boss is heard saying: "It's about time you got married.") (11 sec.)
28. Cut back to the same shot of Jefferies on the phone, with his boss's voice continuing: "Before you turn into a lonesome and bitter old man." Jefferies smiles. (7 sec.)
29. Cut to a closer medium long shot of only two windows of the salesman's apartment. He is undoing his tie, and in the next window we see his wife putting a compress on her forehead. The salesman moves over to her bedroom; camera pans over. He keeps rolling up his sleeves, the wife sits up, they argue, he dismisses her with a shrug. In the meantime, off screen, we still hear Jefferies' phone conversation: "Yeah, can't you just see me rushing home to a hot apartment to listen to the automatic laundry and the electric dishwasher and the garbage disposal and... a nagging wife?" "Jeff, wives don't nag any more—they discuss." "Is that so? Well, maybe in the high-rent district they discuss—in my neighborhood they still nag." "Well, you know best. Call you later." (27 sec.)
30. Cut back to the same medium close-up shot of Jefferies as he finishes his conversation with: "Yeah—have some good news next time, huh?" He puts the receiver down, and looks out. (5 sec.)
31. Cut back to the same shot of the salesman's bedroom window. He keeps shouting, throws down a magazine with fury and walks out toward the other room. (2 sec.)
32. Cut to a wider medium shot of Jefferies, who has an itch inside his cast; he hits the cast with his fist, then reaches for a Chinese wooden back scratcher, inserts it deep into his cast and, with a sense of enormous relief makes funny faces moving the scratcher in and out. He then looks down to the outside. (32 sec.)
33. Cut to a high long shot of the garden area. The salesman comes out from the ground-floor exit door and approaches the rose hedge with his garden tools. (11 sec.)
34. Cut to a long shot of the middle-aged woman, the "sculptress," as she walks out to the garden area and sits down in her chaise longue. Camera follows her, revealing at the same time the alleyway in the background. (6 sec.)
35. Cut back to the same medium close-up of Jefferies looking down;

he lifts himself to see better. (2 sec.)
36. Cut to medium long shot of the sculptress in her chaise longue; she talks with another woman above, who is just putting out her birdcage to the sun. The sculptress settles down to read a magazine. Children playing in the street can be seen via the narrow alleyway. Suddenly, the sculptress gets up and walks over toward the garden, and camera follows her with a pan to the right; she reaches the fence between her house and the garden where the salesman is digging around the rose bushes. She walks up two steps on the fire escape and talks, gesticulating, toward the salesman, protesting, as it seems, his digging or cutting. (24 sec.)
37. Cut to the same shot of Jefferies, half smiling, looking with interest. (2 sec.)
38. Cut to a closer medium long shot of sculptress talking and pointing at salesman. (3 sec.)
39. Cut to closer medium long shot of the salesman talking back to her, roughly; eventually we hear his loud "Shut up" above the street noises. (3 sec.)
40. Cut back to the same medium long shot of the sculptress who, taken aback, walks away, in disdain. (2 sec.)
41. Cut back to the same shot of Jefferies observing the scene. (1.5 sec.)
42. Cut back to the same single shot of the sculptress walking away, visibly upset. (1.5 sec.)
43. Cut back to the same shot of Jefferies, who turns in his chair to respond to a noise at his door. (5 sec.)
44. Cut on action to a long shot, frontal, showing more of the room. We see the visiting Nurse Stella (Thelma Ritter) coming in, she walks over to Jefferies. Camera pans with her to a medium two-shot, she puts her things away, talking all the time; she puts a thermometer in his mouth. "The New York State sentence for a Peeping Tom is six months in the workhouse." Jefferies: "Oh, hello, Stella." Stella: "And they got no windows in the workhouse. You know, in the old days they used to put your eyes out with a redhot poker. Any of those bikini bombshells you're always watchin' worth a redhot poker? Oh, dear, we've become a race of Peeping Toms.

What people ought to do is get outside their own house and look in for a change. Yes, sir. How's that for a bit of homespun philosophy?" Jefferies: "*Reader's Digest,* April 1939." "Well, I only quote from the best." "Yeah. Oh, you don't have to take my temperature this morning." Stella: "See if you can break a hundred. You know, I should have been a gypsy fortune teller instead of an insurance-company nurse. I got a nose for trouble. Smell it 10 miles away. You heard of that stock market crash in '29? I predicted that." (35 sec.)
45. Cut on action to a medium shot from the side (90° angle) two-shot. The nurse busies herself with preparations for the massage, camera follows her as she sets up a couch platform in the foreground. She talks about a scheme she detected with the big insurance company. (15 sec.)
46. Cut to a medium shot of Jefferies (frontal) as he sits in his chair, thermometer in his mouth, talking and teasing the nurse: "Just how'd you do that, Stella?" (3 sec.)
47. Cut to a medium close-up of the nurse preparing a sheet: "Oh—simple. I was nursing a director of General Motors. Kidney ailment, they said. Nerves, I said. Then I asked myself—what's General Motors got to be nervous about? Overproduction, I says. Collapse. When General Motors has to go to the bathroom 10 times a day, the whole country's ready to let go." (23 sec.)
48. Cut back to the same medium shot of Jefferies, looking silly with his thermometer; he takes it out of his mouth and tries, perhaps a little pedantically, to explain to her how the stock market operates: "You know, Stella, in economics, a kidney ailment has no relationship to the stock market. None whatsoever." Stella: "It crashed, didn't it?" (10 sec.)
49. Cut to a full long shot with nurse in the foreground and Jefferies in the background. She goes over to him, takes the thermometer, talks about his looking out the windows; "I can smell trouble right here in this apartment. First you smash your leg, then you get to lookin' out the window—see things you shouldn't see. Trouble. I can see you in court now, surrounded by a bunch of lawyers in double-breasted suits. You're pleading, you say: Judge, it was only a bit of innocent fun. I love my neighbors like a father. And the judge

says: 'Well, congratulations. You've just given birth to three years in Dannemora.'" Jefferies: "Yeah—well, right now, I'd even welcome trouble, you know?" Stella: "You've got a hormone deficiency." Jefferies: "How can you tell from a thermometer?" Stella: "Those bathing beauties you've been watching haven't raised your temperature one degree in a month." Jefferies: "Here we go. One more week. You know, I think you're right. I think there is going to be trouble around here." Stella: "What kind of trouble?" Jefferies: "Lisa Freemont." Stella: "You're kidding? She's a beautiful young girl, and you're a reasonably healthy young man." Camera retreats: We see Jefferies moving forward to the platform, his face, thus, comes closer to the camera (in medium close-up). The nurse behind him starts massaging; he reacts with shivers to the cold cream. (1 min., 19 sec.)
50. *Separation starts*. Cut on action to a close-up of Jefferies, hands folded under his chin. (The nurse is seen only partially—her head is cut off, unless, as she will occasionally do, she leans forward and down to him). Jefferies: "She expects me to marry her." Stella: "That's normal." Jefferies: "I don't want to." Stella: "That's abnormal." Jefferies: "I just... I'm not ready for marriage." (16 sec.)
51. Cut to a close-up of nurse. (Jefferies' head is cut out from frame except for the tip of his head.) She continues the massage and talks: "Every man's ready for marriage when the right girl comes along. And Lisa Freemont's the right girl for any man with half a brain who can get one eye open." (9 sec.)
52. Cut to a close-up of Jefferies as before. "She's all right." (2 sec.)
53. Cut back to close-up of nurse. Stella: "Did you have a fight?" Jefferies (off screen): "No." Stella: "Her father loading up the shot gun?" (3 sec.)
54. Cut back to close-up of Jefferies, as before. He reacts to her simplistic view of things: "What? Please, Stella!" Stella: "It's happened before, you know." (3 sec.)
55. Cut back to close-up of nurse: "Some of the world's best, happiest marriages have started 'under the gun' as you might say." (4 sec.)
56. Cut back to close-up of Jefferies as before; he elaborates: "No, she's just not the girl for me." Stella: "Yeah, she's only perfect." Jefferies: "Well, she's too perfect. She's too talented, she's too beau-

tiful, she's too sophisticated, she's too everything but what I want." Stella: "Is what you want something you can discuss?" Jefferies: "What? Well, it's very simple, Stella. She belongs to that rarefied atmosphere of Park Avenue, you know—expensive restaurants and literary cocktail parties..." Stella: "People with sense belong wherever they're put." Jefferies: "Can you see her traveling around the world with a camera bum who never has more than a week's salary in the bank? If she was only ordinary." *[End of seven-shot separation.]* (7 sec.)

57. Cut on action to a long shot—a two-shot similar to the one in the beginning of the separation. Nurse: "Are you never going to get married?" Jefferies starts getting up with the help of the nurse, he puts his shirt on and talks: "Oh, I'll probably get married, one of these days, but when I do, it's gonna be to someone who thinks of life not just as...just as a new dress and a lobster dinner and the latest scandal. I need a woman who's willing to—hold it—willing to go anywhere and do anything and love it." (22 sec.)

58. Cut on action to a closer medium two-shot. Jefferies, down in his wheelchair, continues: "So the honest thing for me to do is just to call the whole thing off... Let her find somebody else ...." Nurse helps him with the chair, then goes out of frame, camera moves closer to Jefferies. Stella: "Yeah—I can hear you now. Get out of my life, you perfectly wonderful woman! You're too good for me." (10 sec.)

59. *Separation*. Cut to a medium shot of the nurse, putting her bag in order and continuing to philosophize: "Look, Mr. Jefferies: I'm not an educated woman, but I can tell you one thing: When a man and a woman see each other and like each other, they oughta come together—wham—like a coupla taxis on Broadway and not sit around analyzing each other like two specimens in a bottle." Camera follows her. (14 sec.)

60. Cut to medium close-up of Jefferies, pontificating: "There is an intelligent way to approach marriage." (6 sec.)

61. Cut back to the nurse folding the sheet: "Intelligence! Nothing has caused the human race so much trouble as intelligence. Hmpfh! Modern marriage." (9 sec.)

62. Cut back to same medium close-up of Jefferies: "We've progressed emotionally." (3 sec.)
63. Cut back to nurse (same shot). Finishing the folding, she interrupts him: "Once it was see somebody, get excited, get married. Now, it's read a lot of books . . . . " (6 sec.)
64. Cut back to the same shot of Jefferies listening impatiently. Off screen, Stella: "fence with a lot of four syllable words . . . . " (4 sec.)
65. Cut back to nurse (same shot): "psychoanalyze each other until they can't see the difference between a petting party and a civil service exam." (5 sec.)
66. Cut back to the same shot of Jefferies: "People have different emotional levels." He still pontificates. She is off screen interrupting him with the story of her own marriage; she walks over to Jefferies (thus resolving the six-shot separation), forming a two-shot. Jefferies: "Make me a sandwich, please." Stella: "Yes, and I'll put some common sense on the bread. Lisa is the girl for you—marry her." Jefferies: "She pay you much?" The nurse, upset, walks to the back where we assume the kitchen is located. Camera adjusts to center Jefferies in the frame, he smiles and looks out. (35 sec.)
67. Cut to high long shot of the courtyard garden where the salesman is leaving with his garden tools. (3 sec.)
68. Cut back to low medium close-up of Jefferies looking down. (2 sec.)
69. Cut to a long shot of the garden level, where the sculptress is sleeping in her chaise longue. (1.5 sec.)
70. Quick cut to the same shot of Jefferies raising his gaze. (1 sec.)
71. Cut to long shot of the dancer's window, where she is combing her hair. (2 sec.)
72. Cut back to the same low medium close-up of Jefferies as he looks to the right; reacting to a noise of a window going up with a squeak, he leans out to see. (3 sec.)
73. Cut to a medium long shot of a small window, just opened. A couple, dressed as if they have come from their wedding, receive a key from a fat man, who pantomimes that he wishes them well and leaves. The couple are about to kiss when the fat man reappears carrying a valise, bids them good luck and leaves. They kiss. (23 sec.)

74. Cut back to a medium close-up of Jefferies (camera eye level). He smiles while observing. (2 sec.)
75. Cut back to the same framing of the newlyweds pantomime; they end the passionate kiss, the groom opens the front door and calls to bride to follow. (14 sec.)
76. Cut back to the same shot of Jefferies curiously watching. (2 sec.)
77. Cut back to the newlyweds: The groom carries the bride over the threshold into the room, and kisses her as he closes the door with his foot. (6 sec.)
78. Cut back to the same shot of Jefferies; he smiles as if he understands the ritual, satisfied. (3 sec.)
79. Cut back to the newlyweds still kissing. (3 sec.)
80. Cut back to the same shot of Jefferies. He is embarrassed and childishly looks away; he then sneaks a look. (2 sec.)
81. Cut back to newlyweds—they finish kissing, he puts her down, she notices that the shade is up, he walks over and pulls it down. (12 sec.)
82. Cut to a medium two-shot of Jefferies and the nurse both looking: Stella: "Window shopper." *FADE-OUT.* (5 sec.; so far: 15 min., 5 sec.)
83. *FADE-IN.* Sunset. Exterior long shot pan to left, past walls, then the musician's studio; we hear a female's voice practicing scales. Pan over the window, stopping for brief moment by the window of the dancer, who is dressed for the evening, ready to leave. Above the building we see the Manhattan skyline; camera continues to pan by the alleyway with lots of activity on the street, finally coming upon the windowsill of Jefferies' apartment. He is sleeping, medium close-up, then we see a shadow of another face over his, coming slowly. (28 sec.)
84. Cut to the mystery face: It's Lisa (Grace Kelly). She keeps moving closer in to a tight close-up, to the full advantage of her beauty. (2 sec.)
85. Cut to a high close-up of Jefferies' face; he is beginning to wake up. The shadow of Lisa continues to creep up. He looks up, starts to smile. (5 sec.)

86. Cut to a low close-up of Lisa looking at him; she moves closer to an extreme close-up. (3 sec.)
87. Cut on action to a close-up of the two faces in profile. Lisa continues to get closer to him, their lips touch in a mild kiss, then she retreats, yet they remain an inch from each other. Lisa asks quietly: "How's your leg?" Jefferies: "Hurts a little." Lisa: "And your stomach?" Jefferies: "Empty as a football." They kiss again. Lisa: "And your love life?" Jefferies: "Not too active." They kiss. After Lisa: "Anything else bothering you?" Jefferies: "Hmm, hmm...Who are you?" She smiles and withdraws from the frame to the left. Camera makes a round sweep to a frontal view of Jefferies' face (who until now was in profile), ending in wider close-up. (34 sec.)
88. Cut to a low medium shot of Lisa switching on the light of the standing base lamp with a big white shade, saying: "Lisa"; she floats over to the next lamp on a low table also with a shade; she turns that light on too and says: "Carol"; then in a dancing motion she approaches the lamp in the opposite corner of the room and puts that on. By now she is almost in medium long shot. She announces her last name—"Freemont"—and briefly poses, showing her gorgeous full skirt. (13 sec.)
89. Cut to a medium shot of Jefferies: "Is this the Lisa Freemont who never wears the same dress twice?" (4 sec.)
90. Cut to long shot of Lisa, posing like a model and saying: "Only because it is expected of her." She turns around showing her skirt again: "It's right off the Paris plane . . . you think it will sell?" (8 sec.)
91. Cut to the same medium shot of Jefferies, talking with a smirk: "It depends on the quote, you know. Let's see now—there's the plane ticket over and import duties, hidden taxes, profit markups." (5 sec.)
92. Cut to a medium long shot of Lisa as she is taking off her long white gloves: "A steal at $1,100. . . . " (2 sec.)
93. Cut back to the same medium shot of Jefferies: "1,100? Why, they ought to list that skirt on the stock exchange." (7 sec.)
94. Cut back to the same shot of Lisa. She puts her gloves away: "They'll sell a dozen a day in this price range." (2 sec.)
95. Cut back to Jefferies (same shot): "Who buys? Tax collectors?"

(2 sec.)
96. Cut back to Lisa in medium shot: "Even if I had to pay for it, it's worth it . . . just for the occasion . . . big night." (8 sec.)
97. Cut back to same shot of Jefferies: "What is it? I see it's just an ordinary Wednesday . . . the calendar is full of them." (5 sec.)
98. Cut back to the same shot of Lisa, as she puts away her things. "It's the opening night of the last oppressive week of L.B. Jefferies in a cast." (4 sec.)
99. Cut to Jefferies (the same shot): "I didn't notice a big demand for tickets or anything." (4 sec.)
100. Cut to the same shot of Lisa, who walks forward into a medium close-up carrying a small package: "Ah, that's because I bought out the house. You know, this cigarette box has seen better days." (2 sec.)
101. Cut back to Jefferies, a high medium close-up: "Oh, I picked it up in Shanghai; that had also seen better days." (4 sec.)
102. Cut back to the same medium close-up of Lisa: "It's cracked, you never use it . . . I'm sending it to the factory for refinishing." (15 sec.)
103. Cut to the same medium close-up of Jefferies: "Oh, that's no way to spend your hard-earned money." (3 sec.)
104. Cut back to Lisa (same shot): "I want to!" The doorbell rings. She turns to Jefferies asking: "What would you think of starting off with dinner at 21?" She runs to the door; camera follows to a medium long shot. (7 sec.)
105. Cut back to the same medium close-up of Jefferies who asks, "You have perhaps an ambulance downstairs?" (3 sec.)
106. Cut to Lisa in long shot as she steps to the door, turning for a quick glance to Jefferies: "Better than that." She opens the door and announces: "21!" We see a waiter in uniform, red jacket and brass, carrying food and wine. (9 sec.)
107. Cut to a tighter close-up of Jefferies, who looks bewildered. (1.5 sec.)
108. Cut to a medium long shot of both the waiter and Lisa exchanging greetings; the waiter, descending the two steps into the room, says: "Good evening, Mr. Jefferies." He then walks with the

food across the room; Lisa directs him to put the food in the oven, he disappears behind the bookcase and Lisa takes care of the wine and ice. The waiter reappears, helping with the opening of the wine bottle; Lisa gives him money: "This should take care of the taxi." He is on his way: "Thank you, Miss Freemont; have a pleasant dinner, Mr. Jefferies." He departs. (Camera follows his movements.) Lisa closes the door, and camera follows her back to Jefferies' chair. She tells him how busy she was with some clients just back from Paris; she pours the wine. *[End of separation of 18 shots]* (1 min., 14 sec.)
109. Cut to a wide long shot of Jefferies' window, red skyline (a New York sunset) in the background; he sits screen left in profile, Lisa crosses the frame and settles on the right, by the window. She hands him a glass of wine, sips hers and talks fast about her busy schedule: Lunch at 2 with a Mrs. Haywood, two dates and a cocktail party in different parts of the city, and then she changed and ran here to see him. Jefferies, visibly "pulling her leg," asks: "Now, tell me, tell me, what was Mrs. Haywood wearing during the luncheon?" Lisa, unaware, babbles on: "Oh, she had the most divine Italian handprinted skirt. . . . " Jefferies: "Handprinted?" Lisa finally catches on, but controls herself: "To think, I planted three nice items in the column about you today. You cannot buy that kind of publicity;" then adding, "I wish you could open up a studio of your own here." They sip some wine (this is a wide-frame two-shot). Jefferies: "Tell me . . . how would I run it, let's say, from Pakistan . . . . " Lisa moves closer to him: "Jeff, isn't it time you came home . . . you could pick your assignments . . . . " (53 sec.)
[What follows is a series of alternating over-the-shoulder shots.]
110. Cut on action to an over-the-shoulder medium shot from three-quarter profile of Lisa to Jefferies frontal. Jefferies: " . . . You mean I should leave the magazine . . . for what?" (6 sec.)
111. Cut to a reverse over-the-shoulder from three-quarter profile of Jefferies to Lisa frontal. Lisa: "For yourself and me! . . . I could get you a dozen assignments for fashion portraits—now don't laugh. I could do it." (Off screen we hear his voice): "That's what I'm afraid of." (11 sec.)
112. Cut to a reverse over-the-shoulder toward Jefferies: "Can you

see me driving to the fashion salon in my combat boots, in a jeep, with a three-day beard? Would that make a hit?" (8 sec.)
113. Cut to an over-the shoulder toward Lisa: "I can see you looking very handsome and elegant in a dark flannel suit with a striped tie." (5 sec.)
114. Cut to an over-the-shoulder toward Jefferies: "Lisa, let's stop talking nonsense . . . shall we?" (4 sec.)
115. Cut to an over-the-shoulder toward Lisa. She is upset and gets up, crosses the frame and walks out. (3 sec.)
116. Cut to a medium shot of Jefferies, pensive. We see Lisa behind, entering the kitchen area. Jefferies looks out to the window across. (6 sec.)
117. Cut to two lighted windows of the salesman's apartment, his wife is sitting on her bed attending to her makeup—fast pan down to the windows of Lonelyhearts, who finishes fixing her hair, gets up and brushes the front of her dress. (6 sec.)
118. Cut back to the low medium close-up of Jefferies looking down. (1 sec.)
119. Cut to a closer shot, medium long shot, centering on only one of Lonelyheart's windows. She walks over to her kitchen as camera follows from window to window; she picks up a bottle of wine, goes back to dining room (camera follows), lights the candles. A Bing Crosby tune ("To see you is to love you . . . ") plays on the soundtrack. (19 sec.)
120. Cut back to the same shot of Jefferies looking more intensely at Lonelyhearts; we see next to him, in the background, Lisa spreading a tablecloth. (4 sec.)
121. Cut back to Lonelyhearts' same dining-room window. She walks over to her entrance door, as camera pans with her from window to window; she opens the door and steps out to the corridor, where she mimics to a nonexisting person. She invites "him" in and leads him back to the dining room (camera follows) and in pantomime shows him a chair to sit down. (29 sec.)
122. Cut back to the same medium close-up of Jefferies observing the scene with great interest. Lisa is partially seen as she walks back to the kitchen. (3 sec.)

123. Cut back to the same shot of Lonelyhearts, who greets her phantom guest and offers her cheek for a kiss. (7 sec.)
124. Cut back to the same shot of Jefferies reacting, then quickly turning his head back to see if Lisa is around before returning to his observation. (4 sec.)
125. Cut back to the same shot of Lonelyhearts, who serves the wine to her imaginary guest, flirtatiously. (5 sec.)
126. Cut back to the same shot of half-smiling Jefferies. (3 sec.)
127. Cut back to the same shot of Lonelyhearts as she fills the other glass with wine. (2 sec.)
128. Cut back to the same shot of Jefferies, who lifts his own glass of wine. (2 sec.)
129. Cut back to the same shot of Lonelyhearts; she sits down, picks up her glass saluting her companion. (3 sec.)
130. Cut back to the same shot of Jefferies, who also salutes her from his window. (2 sec.)
131. Cut back to the same shot of Lonelyhearts as she sips her wine. (4 sec.)
132. Cut back to the same shot of Jefferies as he too sips his wine. (2 sec.)
133. Cut back to the same shot of Lonelyhearts. She holds her glass up in the air, looks sadly at the empty seat across from her and finally collapses, her head down and her arms outstretched on the table. (19 sec.)
134. Cut to medium two-shot of Jefferies, and Lisa, standing to his right, both looking down. Jefferies: "Miss Lonelyhearts . . . well at least that's something you'll never have to worry about." Lisa: "Can you see my apartment from here, all the way up on 63rd Street?" Jefferies replies: "No, but here we have another apartment." (He looks up.) "You remember Miss Torso?" (17 sec.)
135. Cut to medium long shot of dancer's apartment. Three male visitors are having cocktails, Miss Torso (dancer) among them in an evening low-cut and black dress. Jefferies' voice off screen: "The ballet dancer...she's like a queen bee with her pick of the drones." Miss Torso is filling up the glasses for her guests. (8 sec.)
136. Cut back to the same two-shot. Jefferies laughs, Lisa looks with

interest. (2 sec.)
137. Cut back to same shot of the dancer's party. A man in evening jacket walks out on the balcony and makes an attempt to kiss Miss Torso the moment she walks out to serve him a drink. Lisa, off screen: "I'd say she's doing a woman's hardest job—juggling wolves." (9 sec.)
138. Cut back to the same two-shot of Lisa and Jefferies, looking and smiling. (3 sec.)
139. Cut back to the same shot of the dancer again going out to the balcony; she kisses the man, he wants more; she notices the two men inside the room pointing, and quickly returns to the room; the man follows her. (6 sec.)
140. Cut back to the same two-shot of Lisa and Jefferies. Jefferies: "She picked the most prosperous looking one." Lisa: "She's not in love with any of them!" Jefferies: "How can you see it from here?" Lisa: "You said you can see my apartment on the East Side, didn't you?" She leaves for the kitchen area; camera moves in to a medium close-up of Jefferies, who changes his gaze. (8 sec.)
141. Cut to the small window of the newlyweds—the shade is still down. (2 sec.)
142. Cut back to the same medium close-up of Jefferies, who is disappointed, shrugs and then moves his eyes; somehow resigned, he looks to: (5 sec.)
143. Cut to a long shot of Thorwald's windows. He carries from the kitchen a tray full of food and, crossing from window to window, finally puts it on his sick wife's bed. She sits up, he serves her dinner. (15 sec.)
144. Cut back to the same shot of Jefferies still looking. (2 sec.)
145. Cut to a medium long shot of the bedroom window, in the center. The salesman adjusts his wife's pillow, kisses her on the forehead. She throws some small item off the bed, he picks it up and moves out of the frame. (9 sec.)
146. Cut back to the same medium close-up of Jefferies looking intensely. (4 sec.)
147. Cut to a wider long shot covering two windows of the salesman's apartment. In the left one the salesman is dialing the phone, glancing

to see if his wife is still eating; he pours himself a drink, moves to a soft chair, sits down and starts a phone conversation. In the bedroom (on the right) the wife slowly puts her tray away, and is easing herself out of bed. (22 sec.)

148. Cut back to the same shot of Jefferies looking with great interest. He leans forward, attempting to hear. (4 sec.)

149. Cut to a closer medium long shot of the bedroom window. The wife starts quietly moving to the left to overhear her husband's conversation. Camera moves over toward the other window. First, she is obscured from view by the wall between the windows. Then she sees her husband; he notices her entry. He gets up, puts the phone away with a thump and walks toward her; she backs out (camera follows to the right). Finally, they are both in the bedroom space; he shouts at her, gesticulates and finally, pantomiming a "to hell with you," shrugs and walks out of the room; his reflection is seen in the open window glass. (22 sec.)

150. Cut back to the same shot of Jefferies, thinking about what he saw; then he directs his gaze to the windows across. (3 sec.)

151. Cut to long shot of the musician's studio. He plays on the piano the same tune as before, the film's theme song. A visitor listens (Hitchcock's cameo). (10 sec.)

152. Cut to wider medium close-up of Jefferies; camera starts backing away to a full medium shot as Lisa, with tray, enters, puts it on the table, lights the candle and asks: "Where's that wonderful music coming from?" Jefferies: "Oh, some songwriter over there in the studio apartment. Well! He lives alone. Probably had a very unhappy marriage." Lisa: "Oh, it's enchanting. It's almost as if it were being written especially for us." Lisa starts serving the filet mignon, and lobster, onto his plate. He retorts, snappily: "No wonder he had so much trouble with it." (29 sec.)

153. Cut to a low close-up of Lisa, visibly upset, but under control. "Well, at least you can't say the dinner isn't right," she says with a smile. (5 sec.)

154. Cut to a high medium close-up of Jefferies who, with a smirk on his face, looks at the food and says: "Lisa, it's perfect." (3 sec.)

155. Cut to a close-up of his plate. (1 sec.)

156. Cut to same shot of Jefferies, who continues, "As always." (2 sec.)
157. Cut back to a low medium close-up of Lisa; she sits down, somehow defeated (camera adjusts to a medium close-up of her, as she looks into space). (10 sec.)
FADE-OUT. [Note: What follows is a series of 19 over-the-shoulder shots.]
158. *FADE-IN.* Later in the evening. Medium long shot of Jefferies in three-quarter profile, in his chair. Across from him, over his shoulder, camera points to Lisa, who is reclining on the narrow padding by the window. They continue the same heated argument. Lisa: "There can't be that much difference between people and the way they live. We all eat, talk, drink, laugh, wear clothes. . . . " Jefferies: "Well, now, look—now look. . . . " Lisa: "If you're saying all this because you don't want to tell me the truth, because you're hiding something from me, then maybe I can understand." (12 sec.)
159. Cut to a reverse over-the-shoulder shot toward Jefferies: "I'm not hiding anything. It's just that. . . . " Lisa: "It doesn't make sense! What's so different about it here from over there, or any place you go, that one person couldn't live in both places just as easily?" Jefferies: "Now if you'll just let me explain. . . . " (10 sec.)
160. Cut to a reverse over-the-shoulder toward Lisa, who says: "What is it but traveling from one place to another, taking pictures? It's just like being a tourist on an endless vacation." (6 sec.)
161. Cut to a reverse over-the-shoulder toward Jefferies, who retorts: "Okay. Now that's your opinion. You're entitled to it. Now let me give you my . . . " (6 sec.)
162. Cut to reverse over-the-shoulder toward Lisa. She is dominant, interrupts him, doesn't let him push: "It's ridiculous to say that it can only be done by . . . " (3 sec.)
163. Cut to reverse over-the-shoulder toward Jefferies, saying: "I made a simple statement—a true statement—but I can back it up if you'll just shut up for a minute!" (6 sec.)
164. Cut to reverse over-the-shoulder toward Lisa, snapping back: "If your opinion is as rude as your manner, I don't think I care to hear it." (11 sec.)
165. Cut to reverse over-the-shoulder toward Jefferies: "Oh . . .

Simmer down and listen." (3 sec.)
166. Cut to reverse over-the-shoulder toward Lisa. She boils, upset, mumbling: "You—I can't fit in here—you can't fit in there. I mean, according to you, people should be born, live and die on the same spot." (2 sec.)
167. Cut to reverse over-the-shoulder toward Jefferies. He shouts: "Shut up!" He starts describing in vivid terms the conditions of his work, his various expeditions: "Did you ever eat fish heads and rice?" (4 sec.)
168. Cut to reverse over-the-shoulder toward Lisa: "Of course not." Jefferies' voice: "Well, you might have to if you went with me. Did you ever try to keep warm in a C-54 at 15,200 feet, 20 degrees below zero?" Lisa: "Oh, I do it all the time. Whenever I have a few minutes after lunch." (14 sec.)
169. Cut to reverse over-the-shoulder toward Jefferies, who continues: "Did you ever get shot at? Did you ever get sandbagged at night because somebody got unfavorable publicity from your camera?" (6 sec.)
170. Over-the-shoulder to Lisa; she reacts as Jefferies continues: "Did you ever—those high heels—they'll be great in the jungle . . . and the nylons and those six ounce lingerie." Lisa: "Three!" Jefferies: "All right, three. They'll make a big hit in Finland—just before you freeze to death." Lisa: "Well, if there's one thing I know, it's how to wear the proper clothes." (14 sec.)
171. Over-the-shoulder to Jefferies, who continues: "Yeah—yeah. Well, try and find a raincoat in Brazil—even when it isn't raining. Lisa, in this job you carry one suitcase." (9 sec.)
172. Over-the-shoulder to Lisa listening. Jefferies: "Your home is the available transportation. You don't sleep very much—you bathe less." (4 sec.)
173. Over-the-shoulder to Jefferies, who continues: "And sometimes the food that you eat is made from things that you couldn't even look at when they're alive." (6 sec.)
174. Over-the-shoulder to Lisa: "Jeff, you don't have to be deliberately repulsive just to impress me I'm wrong." Jefferies: "Deliberately repulsive! I'm just trying to make it sound good." (7 sec.)

175. Over-the-shoulder to Jefferies, who continues: "You just have to face it, Lisa, you're not meant for that kind of a life." (5 sec.)
176. Over-the-shoulder to Lisa; she returns hotly and gets up: "You're too stubborn to argue with." Jefferies: "I'm not stubborn—I'm just truthful." Lisa: "I know, a lesser man would have told me it was one long holiday—and I would have been awakened to a rude disillusionment." (17 sec.)
Separation starts.
177. Cut to close-up of Jefferies: "Now, wait a minute. If you want to be vicious about it, I'll be happy to accommodate you." (5 sec.)
178. Cut to medium shot of Lisa; she continues to move away (camera follows her), and she says: "So that's it. You won't stay here, and I cannot go with you?" (11 sec.)
179. Cut to same close-up of Jefferies: "It would be the wrong thing." (4 sec.)
180. Cut to medium shot of Lisa as she reaches for her things. She hesitantly says: "You don't think either one of us could ever change?" (5 sec.)
181. Cut back to the same close-up of Jefferies: "Right now, it doesn't seem so." (3 sec.)
182. Cut to medium long shot of Lisa putting on her long white gloves. She starts toward the door (camera follows her). (13 sec.)
183. Cut to the same close-up of Jefferies looking at her. (1 sec.)
184. Cut to same medium long shot of Lisa as she puts on her white scarf. She says: "I'm in love with you. I don't care what you do for a living. I'd just like to be part of it somehow." (10 sec.)
185. Cut to medium close-up of Jefferies, who turns to follow Lisa's movements. (6 sec.)
186. Cut to same medium long shot of Lisa as she reaches the doorway (camera follows her). (8 sec.)
187. Cut back to medium close-up of Jefferies: "Wait a minute." (4 sec.)
188. Cut to medium long shot of Lisa as she opens the door. (4 sec.)
189. Cut to medium long shot of Jefferies as he turns and wheels quickly forward to a medium close-up: "Now Lisa . . . couldn't we have a status quo?" (5 sec.)

190. Cut to medium shot of Lisa opening the door farther and turning to him. (3 sec.)
191. Cut back to medium close-up of Jefferies: "When am I going to see you again?" (3 sec.)
192. Cut back to medium shot of Lisa, saying hesitantly: "Not for a long time." Then, after a pause: "At least not until tomorrow night." The door closes. *No resolution of the separation.* (8 sec.)
193. Cut to medium close-up of Jefferies in profile. He is thinking, and turns his wheelchair. (12 sec.)
194. Cut on action to a frontal medium shot of Jefferies as he continues turning the wheelchair, visibly tortured by what has happened; he then looks through his window across. (9 sec.)
195. Cut to camera panning, starting with the alleyway from left to right in full long shot of the exterior right view of the windows; then, a quick pan left and up to the balcony when *a sudden scream is heard*. (15 sec.)
196. Cut to a medium close-up of Jefferies reacting to the noise. *FADE-OUT.* (9 sec.)
197. *FADE-IN* to medium shot (frontal) of Jefferies sleeping in his wheelchair (later same night). (6 sec.)
198. Cut to exterior night long shot of the balcony across; it starts raining. (5 sec.)
199. Cut to closer medium close-up of Jefferies waking up, looking out across. (5 sec.)
200. Cut to closer medium long shot of the fire escape; rain comes down harder. The couple sleeping outside get out from under their sheets and start to drag their mattresses and bedding inside in a hurry. (12 sec.)
201. Cut to same medium close-up of Jefferies reacting with a smile. (2 sec.)
202. Cut back to same medium long shot of the fire escape. The couple continue frantically to gather their bedding. (3 sec.)
203. Cut back to same medium close-up of Jefferies, who smiles. (2 sec.)
204. Cut back to same medium long-shot of the fire escape. The couple push their mattresses through the window into the apart-

ment, and the man dives in the same way. (7 sec.)
205. Cut to the small window in the entrance hall of the raincoat-clad traveling salesman, who is locking his door and leaving down the corridor. (9 sec.)
206. Cut back to same medium close-up of Jefferies. He is curious, trying to figure out the meaning of it. He changes his gaze down to: (10 sec.)
207. Cut to a long shot of the alleyway, where he sees the salesman walking through with a heavy valise in hand. The street is wet, and automobiles pass by. (8 sec.)
208. Cut back to same medium close-up of Jefferies, who is watching intensely, then checks his watch. (5 sec.)
209. Insert close-up of wristwatch. It's 1:50 a.m. *FADE-OUT.* (3 sec.)
210. *FADE-IN* on same close-up of the wristwatch. It's 2:35 a.m. (3 sec.)
211. Cut to medium shot of Jefferies looking at the watch. (3 sec.)
212. Cut to the salesman returning to his door with the same valise, but much lighter. He enters his apartment. (10 sec.)
213. Cut to same medium close-up of Jefferies looking worried. He suddenly looks up to: (4 sec.)
214. Cut to musician's studio as the lights go on. The drunk musician enters his room, tossing around in stupor. (9 sec.)
215. Cut to same medium close-up of Jefferies looking on. (2 sec.)
216. Cut back to long shot of the musician's studio. He is trying to play the piano. Standing, he reels and sweeps away his sheet music down from the piano, and falls down against the rear wall. (6 sec.)
217. Cut to wider medium shot of Jefferies, who smiles and slowly settles himself back to sleep; still, he notices something across. (9 sec.)
218. Cut back to same shot of the salesman's corridor. He leaves again with the same heavy valise down the corridor. (6 sec.)
219. Cut back to same medium shot of Jefferies wondering and puzzled. (5 sec.)
220. Quick cut to the empty corridor. (1 sec.)
221. Cut to familiar long shot of the alleyway, with the salesman

crossing into the street. The rain is heavy. Sounds of thunder. It's stormy outside. (6 sec.)
222. Cut back to same medium shot of Jefferies, who's very preoccupied, not understanding. (9 sec.)
FADE-OUT.
223. *FADE-IN* to close-up of Jefferies sleeping. Slowly, he wakes up, and he looks across. (8 sec.)
224. Cut to salesman's windows, where all shades are down; camera pans left to the empty corridor. (6 sec.)
225. Cut back to same close-up of Jefferies, who's taking a drink. (3 sec.)
226. Cut to long shot of the empty alleyway. Only passing cars are on the street. Camera pans up to the dancer's apartment as the lights inside go on. She has just entered and is struggling to close her door on a stubborn companion whom she won't let in. (4 sec.)
227. Cut to same close-up of Jefferies looking, interested. (3 sec.)
228. Cut back to long shot of dancer's apartment. She finally succeeds in shutting the door. Dressed in a strapless evening gown, she turns and walks forward toward her window, and she displays herself at the window. (24 sec.)
229. Cut to same close-up of Jefferies, who watches with interest. Then he turns his line of vision. (4 sec.)
230. Cut to a long shot of the alleyway, where he sees again the salesman coming back with the valise. The camera pans up to the dancer's window, panning right to the salesman's corridor as he approaches his door with key in hand, opens it and enters. (20 sec.)
231. Cut back to Jefferies' close-up as he watches with difficulty, fighting back his sleepiness, without success. (9 sec.)
232. Cut to long shot of the dancer's window as she turns off her lights. Camera pans to the right to the salesman's windows, where the shades are down, as before. (7 sec.)
FADE-OUT.
233. *FADE-IN* on Jefferies in close-up as he sleeps in his wheelchair. Camera pans to the right over the building, passing over the salesman's windows; it stops at his corridor as he is leaving in the company of a woman in black. Camera continues panning, this time

to the left, eventually reaching Jefferies in close-up, still sleeping. (27 sec.)
FADE-OUT. Note: The composer's new tune becomes the melody of the film, and is heard throughout the above section.
234. *FADE-IN* next day (strong theme music) to exterior day long shot of the ground-floor level with view on the alleyway. The sculptress is attending to one of her pieces, an abstract bust. A man is delivering a block of ice. (34 sec.)
235. Cut on action to close medium long shot of the man passing with the block of ice on his shoulder, exchanging a greeting with the sculptress. Camera pans up to the dancer's window; in passing she can be seen dancing vigorously. Camera continues panning up to the fire-escape platform, from which a woman is lowering her dog in a basket; camera pans down with the basket until the dog lands in the garden; then a dramatic pan, almost a swish, to the left, ending well inside Jefferies' room, where the nurse is in the process of massaging his back. They both are in medium shot profile. (30 sec.)
236. Cut on action to frontal medium shot of the nurse and Jefferies. She talks while massaging, jokingly remarking that "the insurance company would be much happier if he would sleep in his bed instead of in his chair." She knows that he watches the windows across all night. He admits and gives her the news, window by window. He tells her about the mysterious comings and goings of the salesman, all during the stormy night, saying "I just...I just can't figure it. He went out several times last night in the rain, carrying his sample case." Stella: "Well, he's a salesman, isn't he?" Jefferies: "Well, what would he be selling at three o'clock in the morning?" Stella: "Flashlights. Luminous dials for watches. House numbers that light up." Jefferies: "I don't think so. I think he was taking somethin' out of the apartment." Stella: "Uh-huh! His personal effects. He's gonna run out on her, the coward." Jefferies: "Yeah, yeah. Sometimes it's worse to stay than it is to run." Stella: "Yeah—well it takes a particularly low type of man to do a thing like that." Finally, Jefferies gets up, and with the help of the nurse, gets to his chair in the corner by the window. The camera adjusts in the process with an elaborate side movement. Stella asks: "How about this morning? Any further

developments?" Jefferies: "No, the shades were all drawn in the apartment." Stella: "In this heat? Well they're up." Camera follows as she moves closer to his chair. They look. (1 min. 47 sec.)
237. Cut to long shot of the salesman's window; he is looking out. (2 sec.)
238. Cut back to the same medium shot of the nurse and Jefferies, who says: "Get back, quickly"; he starts moving his chair back. (4 sec.)
239. Cut back to the same shot of salesman at his window looking down to the yard. (2 sec.)
240. Cut back to the same two-shot (medium shot) of the nurse and Jefferies, who says: "It's not an ordinary look . . . the man behaves as if he is afraid someone is watching him. . . . " (5 sec.)
241. Cut back to same shot, but closer (medium long shot), of the salesman; he notices something, and kneels down by the window to get closer to the glass. (4 sec.)
242. Cut to medium close-up of Jefferies wheeling himself closer to his window, looking across. (8 sec.)
243. Cut to a long shot of salesman's window, who still looks down; camera pans down to the garden, where the little dog is smelling out the soil where the salesman worked the day before. (4 sec.)
244. Cut back to same medium close-up of Jefferies, looking cautiously. (3 sec.)
245. Cut to medium long shot of fire-escape stairway; the lady calls her dog back. He obeys and jumps into his basket. (5 sec.)
246. Cut back to medium close-up of Jefferies, smiling. In the back, the nurse is getting ready to leave, mumbling: "See you tomorrow." He hardly reacts. (9 sec.)
247. Cut to full long shot of the salesman's windows. He is busy cleaning his valise. (3 sec.)
248. Cut back to same medium close-up of Jefferies, observing the salesman's activity. Camera pulls back, the nurse is by the door. Jefferies turns around his wheelchair, asks her to hand him his field glasses, which are hanging by the door. She grudgingly obliges, complaining: "And don't sleep in that chair again." "Trouble. I can smell it. I'll be glad when they crack that cast and I can get out of here." She

leaves the room as camera adjusts to Jefferies (back in medium close-up) lifting his field glasses (momentarily a reflection of the wall across and the windows is seen in the lenses as the camera moves in closer to a close-up of Jefferies and his field glasses). (10 sec.)
249. Cut to closer medium shot (justified by the field glasses' magnification) of the window behind which the salesman is clearly seen scouring his display case, replacing the plastic, closing the valise and putting it down. (12 sec.)
250. Cut back to same close-up of Jefferies lowering his glasses, worried that he might have, by chance, been seen; he cautiously moves his wheelchair back (he is now in a medium close-up) into the shadow, lifts his glasses. (12 sec.)
251. Cut back to same medium shot of the salesman, apparently not suspecting anything, walking over to his kitchen window (as camera follows), opening a cabinet. (8 sec.)
252. Cut back to same medium close-up of Jefferies, who puts away his field glasses, reaches to a cabinet below, pulls out a giant telephoto lens and fits it on his 35mm reflex camera; he then wheels himself forward (into the light), resting his lens on his knee ready to look or take a shot. (Again, we see a momentary reflection of the salesman's windows in the big lens.) *Note: real time action without a cut.* (1 min., 5 sec.)
253. Cut to close shot (medium shot) of the kitchen window, where the salesman is wrapping a narrow-bladed 1 $^{1}/_{2}$-foot-long hand saw and a large knife into newspapers; he then takes the package to the other room. (18 sec.)
254. Cut back to medium close-up of Jefferies as he lowers the camera from his eye, looks, then again lifts the lens into viewing position. (6 sec.)
255. Cut back to medium shot of the salesman stretching and yawning. He then walks over to his living room window, takes off his glasses and lowers himself to a couch by the window (out of view.) (10 sec.)
256. Cut back to close-up of Jefferies slowly lowering his lens enough to see his eyes moving thoughtfully from left to right. (An idea is born in his mind.) (9 sec.)

FADE-OUT.
257. *FADE-IN.* Evening, close-up of a thermometer showing 82°F, then quick pan to long shot of musician's studio. He is scrubbing his floor, shirtless. He stops for a moment, plays a few chords on the piano and then is back to the floor. Camera pans to the left and up to a long shot of the balcony, where a child is fitted out into a night shirt; camera continues panning to upper fire escape, where the couple are setting up their mattresses and the woman whistles for her dog. (32 sec.)
258. Camera pans down to the garden as the dog jumps into its basket, pans up via the dancer's bathroom window (we see only her head), passing the sculptress, finally reaching Jefferies' window, where he and Lisa, in a medium close-up, are kissing. (29 sec.)
259. Cut on action to closer and higher shot of the two (close-up) kissing, Jefferies occasionally talking and Lisa kissing and interrupting him: Lisa: "How far does a girl have to go before you notice her?" Jefferies: "Well, if she's pretty enough she doesn't have to go anywhere. She just has to be." "Well, ain't I? Pay attention to me." Jefferies: "Well, I'm not on the other side of the room." She caresses him. Lisa: "Your mind is. And when I want a man I want all of him." Jefferies: "Don't . . . don't you ever have any problems?" They kiss again. Lisa: "I have one now." She hugs him. Jefferies: "So do I." Lisa: "Tell me about it." Jefferies: "Why, why should a man leave his apartment three times on a rainy night with a suitcase? And come back three times?" Lisa: "He likes the way his wife welcomes him home." She kisses him. Jefferies: "Oh. No, no—no. No, no—not—not this salesman's wife. And why didn't he go to work today?" Lisa: "Homework. It's more interesting." Jefferies: "What's more interesting about a butcher knife and a small saw, wrapped in newspaper, hun?" Lisa: "Nothing, thank heaven." Jefferies: "Why hasn't he been in his wife's bedroom all day?" Lisa: "I wouldn't dare answer that." Jefferies and Lisa kiss. She puts her head on his shoulder. Jefferies goes on: "There must be something wrong . . . What do you think?" Lisa, annoyed, gets up and out of his embrace; she says, ironically: "There must be something wrong with me!" (37 sec.)

260. Cut to medium shot of Lisa as she fixes her hair. *Separation starts*. (3 sec.)
261. Cut on movement to high medium shot of Lisa. She settles down on the bench by the window, teasing him: Lisa: "Something too frightful to utter." (3 sec.)
262. Cut to medium shot of Jefferies talking, totally absorbed: "He went out a few minutes ago in his undershirt—he hasn't come back yet."(3 sec.)
263. Cut to same medium shot of Lisa, reclined, as she gets hold of a cigarette and starts smoking. (3 sec.)
264. Cut back to same medium shot of Jefferies looking out. (3 sec.)
265. Cut to high long shot of the dancer's window; she is on her bed reading (a bit longer duration shot). (9 sec.)
266. Cut back to same medium shot of Jefferies; he thinks, then says: "It must be terrible to tackle." (3 sec.)
267. Cut back to same medium shot of Lisa, wondering. (2 sec.)
268. Cut back to same medium shot of Jefferies: "Just how would you start to cut up a human body." (5 sec.)
269. Cut back to same medium shot of Lisa, smoking. She lifts herself, lights the lamp next to her and says: "Jeff, I'll be honest with you, you're beginning to scare me a little." (7 sec.)
270. Cut back to same medium shot of Jefferies as he looks out intensely. (1 sec.)
271. Cut back to same medium shot of Lisa, who starts: "Jeff, did you hear what I said?" (3 sec.)
272. Cut back to same medium shot of Jefferies, who interrupts her: "Sssh, he's coming back." (3 sec.)
273. Cut back to same medium shot of Lisa, who turns to look out. (2 sec.)
274. Cut to long shot of salesman's window in the corridor. He comes in holding a heavy rope, enters the apartment and passes through windows to the bedroom, where the venetian blinds are down. (12 sec.)
275. Cut back to same medium shot of Jefferies, who grabs his field glasses, pointing them across. (3 sec.)
276. Cut to medium long shot of the shaded window; the silhouette

of the salesman is visible, moving around. (9 sec.)
277. *Separation resolved.* Cut to medium long shot of Jefferies with Lisa, her back to the camera; Jefferies is still looking through his field glasses. She comes around him, turns his wheelchair away from the window and takes his field glasses from him. She delivers an energetic sermon: "The way you look into people's windows is sick." He defends himself: "What's the matter?" Lisa: "Sitting around, looking out of the window to kill time is one thing—but doing it the way you are, with binoculars and wild opinions about every little thing you see is . . . is diseased!" Jefferies: "Well, do you think I consider it recreation?" Lisa: "I don't know what you consider it, but if you don't stop it, I'm getting out of here!" Jefferies: "Well, what the . . . . " Lisa: "What is it you're looking for?" Jefferies: "I just want to find out what's the matter with the salesman's wife, that's all. Does that make me sound like a madman?" Lisa: "What makes you think there's something the matter with her?" Jefferies: "A lot of things. She's an invalid—she demands constant care—and yet neither the husband nor anyone else has been in to see her all day. Why?" Camera follows Lisa's movements in a medium shot as she tries to walk away: Lisa: "Maybe she died." Jefferies: "Where's the doctor? Where's the undertaker?" (43 sec.)
278. Cut to medium shot of Jefferies, who wheels himself toward Lisa—camera follows—ending in a medium two-shot of profiles. Lisa insists that the wife might be sleeping. Jefferies argues that strange things were going on in that household. She prevents him from returning to his station: "There is nothing to see." He insists: "Why, there is something. I've seen it through that window. I've seen bickering and family quarrels and mysterious trips at night and knives and saws and rope—and now since last evening, not a sign of the wife. All right, now you tell me where she is and what she's doing." Lisa: "I don't know." Jefferies: "Where is she?" Lisa: "Maybe he's leaving his wife, I don't know—I don't care! Lots of people have knives and saws and ropes around their houses. And lots of men don't speak to their wives all day. Lots of wives nag and men hate them, and trouble starts—but very, very few of them end up in murder, if that's what you're thinking." Jefferies: "It's pretty hard for

you to keep away from that word, isn't it, huh?" Lisa: "You could see all that he did, couldn't you?" Jefferies: "Of course, I . . . . " "You could see while the shades are up . . . . " (46 sec.)
279. Cut to closer medium shot of the two. Lisa kneels next to him, explaining the foolishness of his hypothesis: "Oh, Jeff, do you think a murderer would let you see all that?" That he wouldn't pull the shades down and hide behind them?" Jefferies: "Just where he's being clever. He's being nonchalant about things." (11 sec.)
280. Cut to medium over-the-shoulder shot toward Lisa. She insists that a murderer would not parade his crimes in front of an open window. Jefferies: "Why not?" Lisa: "I bet that there might be something more interesting behind those windows." She points to the newlyweds' shaded window. Jefferies turns to see. (13 sec.)
281. Cut to medium shot of the small window with the shade down (as before). Camera pans to left to a low close-up of Jefferies, who smiles: "No comment." (7 sec.)
282. Cut to close-up of Lisa; she gets up from her crouching position, camera moves up with her (dramatically). (6 sec.)
283. Cut to medium close-up of Jefferies, who follows her getting up with his eyes. (1 sec.)
284. Cut to medium shot of the two (frontal). Both look intensely across as if something has happened. Jefferies energetically moves his chair around and to the window, leaving Lisa out of frame. She quickly rejoins him by reentering the frame; he picks up his field glasses. (8 sec.)
285. Cut to medium shot of the salesman's window, this time open and shadeless. The ropes are around the big sea trunk; the salesman wipes his forehead. (6 sec.)
286. Cut back to same medium shot of Jefferies and Lisa. Camera moves in at a good pace to a low close-up of Lisa (alone). She's transfigured: "Let's start from the beginning, Jeff, tell me everything you saw . . . and . . . what it . . . means." (12 sec.)
FADE-OUT.
287. *FADE-IN* (late evening). Tight close-up of a hand on a black phone receiver. (3 sec.)
288. Cut to tight close-up of Jefferies' face. He seems to be waiting

for a call. (3 sec.)
289. Cut to medium long shot of the salesman's three windows; in the dark, a flashlight is seen in the room. (2 sec.)
290. Cut back to same close-up of Jefferies. The phone rings. Lisa is on the line. "The name on the second-floor rear mailbox reads Mr. and Mrs. Lars—that's L-A-R-S—Lars Thorwald." Jefferies: "What's the number of the apartment house?" Lisa: "One-two-five West Ninth Street." Jefferies: "Thank you, dear." Lisa: "Okay, Chief. What's my next assignment?" Jefferies: "Just go home." Lisa: "All right—but what's he doing now?" Jefferies: "He's just sitting in the living room. In the dark. Hasn't gone near the bedroom. All right, now you go home and get some sleep now. Goodnight." Lisa's voice: "Goodnight." (41 sec.)
291. Cut to the same shot of the three windows; in the dark a cigarette gleams inside the dining room. (6 sec.)
FADE-OUT.
292. *FADE-IN.* Morning. A wide medium shot of Jefferies in his chair talking on the phone. In the background, the nurse is busily preparing breakfast. She comes and goes out of frame. Jefferies is talking to an old friend, Doyle, a detective, asking him urgently to come over. The detective defends himself, by saying that "this is my day off." Jefferies: "So what, I did my best pictures on my day off." Apparently, he promises to come. Jefferies puts down the receiver. Nurse comes into the frame with a plate. She looks to the window and talks about the "murder." Nurse: "You called the police?" Jefferies explains that it's far less formal—a friend of his happens to be a detective. "Just where do you suppose he cut her up? Of course—the bathtub! That's the only place where he could have washed away the blood." Jefferies is about to eat his bacon. The scene is comical, with a sprinkle of the morbid as Jefferies tries to eat. (1 min., 10 sec.)
293. Cut to medium long shot of Thorwald's two windows. Cigarette smoke is seen in the dining room. (3 sec.)
294. Cut back to two-shot of Jefferies and the nurse, who says: "He better take that trunk away before it starts to leak." Jefferies practically chokes on his coffee. Nurse leaves the frame, Jefferies looks out. (12 sec.)

295. Cut to medium long shot of the dancer's balcony. She is at the clothesline hanging up her panties next to her bra, continuously dancing, practicing her hip movements. (4 sec.)
296. Cut to same medium shot of Jefferies; he smiles, then changes his gaze to: (1 sec.)
297. The newlyweds' little shaded window in a medium shot. (2 sec.)
298. Cut back to same medium shot of Jefferies, pleased and smiling; he moves forward. (3 sec.)
299. Cut back to medium shot of the little window. The "groom," clad in a T-shirt, lifts the shade and leans out for fresh air. His wife's voice calls him back: "Ha-rr-y." (9 sec.)
300. Cut back to same medium shot of Jefferies, who smiles with understanding. The nurse enters his frame from behind calling out: "Look, look." (4 sec.)
301. Cut to long shot of Thorwald's windows. (The comic relief of the last few cuts is dispelled.) Two uniformed parcel-post men enter the apartment with Thorwald, who leads them to the bedroom, where a big trunk, all roped, is ready to be moved. Thorwald signs the shipping papers. (11 sec.)
302. Cut back to medium shot of Jefferies and the nurse behind him. Jefferies grabs the field glasses and looks. (4 sec.)
303. Cut to closer medium shot of the window across. Thorwald hands the parcel-post men the signed papers. They pick up the trunk and start for the door as camera follows them from window to window into the corridor. (22 sec.)
304. Cut back to same medium shot of the nurse and Jefferies, who worries about "losing them the moment the truck leaves." Stella runs to the door. Jefferies: "Don't do anything foolish." Stella: "I'll just get the name of the truck firm." She leaves, and camera pans back to Jefferies, who resumes his observations with the field glasses. (12 sec.)
305. Cut to close medium long shot of the alleyway with traffic in the street. Camera swish pans to the right and up to the living room window of Thorwald, who picks up the phone and dials. He relaxes back into his armchair to talk. (12 sec.)

306. Cut to close-up of Jefferies with his glasses. (2 sec.)
307. Cut back to same medium shot of Thorwald talking on the phone. (2 sec.)
308. Cut back to same close-up of Jefferies, who momentarily takes down his field glasses, then looks around and down as if searching. (4 sec.)
309. Cut to medium long shot of the alleyway. A truck passes, then the nurse steps back into view, and looks intensely. (4 sec.)
310. Cut back to same close-up of Jefferies with field glasses. (2 sec.)
311. Cut to closer (via the field glasses) medium long shot of the nurse in the alleyway, gesticulating to Jefferies that she apparently missed the truck. (4 sec.)
312. Cut back to same close-up of Jefferies. He is disappointed and at a loss. (5 sec.)
FADE-OUT.
313. *FADE-IN.* Late in the day. Wide long shot of two men with their backs to the camera looking out the window: Jefferies on the left, his detective friend, Doyle (Wendel Corey), on the right. They use the field glasses. Across is the building with all the familiar windows. (9 sec.)
314. Cut to medium shot of the two. The detective, still with his back to the camera: "You didn't see the killing or the body? How do you know there was a murder?" (9 sec.)
315. Cut to a medium shot of the above. The detective (now facing the camera) is pessimistic about the whole affair. Jefferies: "Because everything this fellow's done has been suspicious. Trips at night in the rain, and knives and saws and trunks with rope, and now this wife that isn't there any more." (36 sec.)
316. Cut to an over-the-shoulder medium two-shot toward Jefferies. Doyle: "I admit it all has a mysterious sound. It could be a number of things. Murder's the least possible." (7 sec.)
317. Cut to over-the-shoulder medium shot toward the detective, who continues: "It's too obvious and stupid a way to commit murder—in full view of 50 windows? And then sit over there smoking a cigar—waiting for the police to pick him up?" (4 sec.)
318. Cut to over-the-shoulder medium shot towards Jefferies, who

asks: "You think I made all that up?" Detective: "Not necessarily, it might have a very simple explanation." (6 sec.)
319. Cut to over-the-shoulder medium shot toward the detective. Jefferies: "For instance?" Detective: "Like a trip." Jefferies: "His wife was sick in bed." The detective gets up after consulting his watch, and walks away; camera follows him to the door, he turns and says: "I'll do some poking of my own." (16 sec.)
320. Cut to medium shot of Jefferies, facing camera: "Thank you very much." (2 sec.)
321. Cut to medium shot of the detective. He promises to find out whether the wife left and to where. (9 sec.)
322. Cut to tighter medium close-up of Jefferies. The detective asks, off screen: "Do you have any headaches lately?" Jefferies tries to answer: "Not. . . " (2 sec.)
323. Cut back to same medium shot of the detective, who suspects (with irony) that Jefferies perhaps hallucinated. (5 sec.)
324. Cut back to same medium close-up of Jefferies, who is about to say something, then gives up and looks through the window. (5 sec.)
325. Cut to high long shot of the garden, where the little dog is sniffing around the roses. (2 sec.)
326. Cut back to same medium close-up of Jefferies turning his wheel-chair closer to the window. (2 sec.)
327. Cut back to same long shot of the garden, where the dog is scratching the ground close to the rose bush. (1 sec.)
328. Cut back to same medium close-up of Jefferies, smiling. (2 sec.)
329. Cut back to same shot of the dog, scratching. We see Thorwald coming down to the garden with watering can and tools. He approaches the dog, pats him and gently sends him on his way. (10 sec.)
330. Cut back to same medium close-up of Jefferies, looking. (1 sec.)
331. Cut back to same long shot of the garden. Thorwald pushes the earth around the rose plant with his foot. (2 sec.)
332. Cut back to same medium close-up of Jefferies. He wonders abut the meaning of what he sees. He moves his gaze to the left. (6 sec.)

333. Cut to medium long shot of the alleyway. The detective is standing, hands in his trouser pockets, then leaves. (8 sec.)
FADE-OUT.
334. *FADE-IN.* Later in the day. Full long shot of Jefferies' room, with detective Doyle on the left and Jefferies on the right. Doyle gives him a terse report: "He has a six-months' lease—used up a little more than five and a half months of it. He's quiet—drinks, but not to drunkenness. Pays his bills promptly, with money earned as a costume jewelry salesman—wholesale. Kept to himself. None of his neighbors got close to him or his wife." Jefferies: "Yeah, well, I think they missed their chance with her." Doyle: "She never left the apartment. . . . " Jefferies: "Then where is she—in the icebox?" Doyle: "Until yesterday morning." Jefferies: "What time?" Doyle: "Six a.m. . . . " Jefferies: "Six a.m. I think that's about the time I fell asleep." The detective, with a drink in his hand, moves closer to Jefferies, into a medium two-shot, camera follows. Doyle: "Too bad. The Thorwalds were leaving the apartment house at just about that time. Feel a little foolish?" Jefferies: "No, not yet." They both look out the window. (14 sec.)
335. Cut to medium long shot [*Separation starts*] of the dancer's balcony. She still exercises. (2 sec.)
336. Cut to medium close-up of the detective, smiling. (2 sec.)
337. Cut to medium shot of Jefferies, who looks disappointed, and turns to the detective: "How's your wife?" (5 sec.)
338. Cut back to same medium close-up of the detective: "Oh, she's fine." Detective is still looking through the window; he turns away. (5 sec.)
339. Cut back to same shot of Jefferies: "Who said they left?" (3 sec.)
340. Cut back to closer medium close-up of the detective who quickly turns back: Doyle: "Oh, the building superintendent and two tenants. Flat statements—no hesitation—they jibed to the letter. The Thorwalds were on their way to the railroad station." (11 sec.)
341. Cut back to same medium close-up of Jefferies: "Now, how could anyone guess that? Did they have signs on the luggage saying Grand Central?" (8 sec.)

342. Cut to medium shot of the detective, pouring himself more whiskey and explaining that Thorwald put his wife on a train to the country. (6 sec.)
343. Cut to same medium close-up of Jefferies: "I see . . . pretty convenient. . . . Can the super check those statements?" (6 sec.)
344. Cut to same medium shot of the detective: "Huh?" (2 sec.)
345. Cut back to same medium close-up of Jefferies who, excited, persists: "What good can that information be? . . . It's a second-hand version of an unsupported statement of the murderer himself. . . Did anyone actually see the wife get off the train?" (11 sec.)
346. Cut to same shot of the detective. Doyle: "I have to remind you that you stated it yourself...by stating that she was murdered." (4 sec.)
347. Cut back to same shot of Jefferies, trying to say something. (2 sec.)
348. Cut back to the same shot of the detective, making a step forward asking: "Now...did you actually see her murdered?" (2 sec.)
349. Cut back to same medium close-up of Jefferies: "What are you doing? . . . Solving a case or are you trying to make me look foolish?" (7 sec.)
350. Cut to medium close-up of Doyle: "Well, if possible, both." (3 sec.)
351. Cut back to same medium close-up of Jefferies, gesturing with his back-scratcher while talking: "Well, then do a good job of it; go over there and search Thorwald's apartment. It must be knee-deep in evidence." (7 sec.)
352. Cut to Doyle, pacing across the room as camera pans in medium shot: "I can't do that, even if he isn't there." (5 sec.)
353. Cut back to same medium close-up of Jefferies: "What's he have? Does he have a courtesy card from the police department or something?" (5 sec.)
354. Cut back to same medium shot of the detective: "Now, don't get me mad. Not even a detective can walk into an apartment and search it. Why, if I were caught in there, they'd have my badge within 10 minutes." (1 sec.)
355. Cut back to same medium close-up of Jefferies: "All right, make

sure you don't get caught, that's all. But if you find something, you've got a murderer and they don't care anything about a coupla house rules. If you don't find anything, the fellow's clear." (8 sec.)
356. Cut back to same medium shot of the detective: "At the risk of sounding stuffy, I'd like to remind you of the Constitution, and the phrase search . . . " (6 sec.)
357. Cut back to same shot of Jefferies. Doyle continues off screen: "warrant, issued by a judge who knows his Bill of Rights verbatim. He must ask for evidence." Jefferies: "Give him evidence." (6 sec.)
358. Cut back to same medium shot of Doyle. He sits down comfortably in a chair. (18 sec.)
359. Cut back to same medium close-up of Jefferies, who desperately says: "You know, by tomorrow morning there may not be any evidence at all left in that apartment, you know that." (5 sec.)
360. Cut back to same medium shot of the detective: "Right, man." (3 sec.)
361. Cut back to same medium close-up of Jefferies: "Well, what. . . what do you need before you can search? Tell me now, what do you need. . . bloody footsteps leading up to the door?" (6 sec.)
362. Cut back to same medium shot of Doyle: "One thing I don't need is heckling. You called me and asked for help. Now, you're behaving like a taxpayer." He gets up and looks at his watch: "How could we stand each other in that plane for two years during the war? I can't understand." (11 sec.)
363. Cut back to same medium close-up of Jefferies, sulking. (2 sec.)
364. Cut back to same medium shot of the detective. He is ready to leave: "Well, I guess I'll go to the railroad station and check on Thorwald's story." (6 sec.)
365. Cut back to same shot of Jefferies: "Forget the story; find the trunk." (4 sec.)
366. Cut back to same medium shot of the detective. He's at the door, and, remembering, says, "Oh, by the way," and takes a note out of his pocket: "Here's a postcard from Thorwald's mailbox: Arrived, feeling better, Anna. (18 sec.)
367. Cut back to same shot of Jefferies, who listens, stunned: "Is Anna who I think it is?" (8 sec.)

368. Cut back to same medium shot of the detective at the door: "Yes. Mrs. Thorwald." (2 sec.)
369. Cut back to medium shot of Jefferies; he hits his chair arm with the backscratcher, resigned. (3 sec.)
370. Cut to same medium shot of the detective: "You need anything?" (3 sec.)
371. Cut back to same medium shot of Jefferies: "No, I need a detective." (2 sec.)
372. Cut to same shot of the detective as he leaves. (4 sec.)
373. Cut to wider medium long shot of Jefferies, his toes sticking out of the cast in the foreground. He tries to reach his toes with the scratcher, finally feeds the scratcher deep under the cast and, with a sigh of relief, succeeds in calming the itch. *End of the Separation* (17 sec.)
FADE-OUT.
374. *FADE-IN.* Later in the evening. Close-up of the telephoto lens. A hand reaches for a sandwich. Camera follows the hand to Jefferies' face as he starts eating the sandwich. He also looks out. (11 sec.)
375. Cut to long shot of the windows across. The little dog is being lowered to the garden, camera follows down, dog jumps out; camera pans to the right over to the window of Miss Lonelyhearts, who has just finished putting on her makeup, with a small mirror in her hand. (16 sec.)
376. Cut to close shot of Jefferies, who puts down sandwich and picks up camera. (5 sec.)
377. Cut to medium shot of Miss Lonelyhearts (via the telephoto lens). She has her glasses on, is doing the final makeup touches, puts her glasses away, checks in the small mirror, puts her glasses on again, corrects her lipstick, puts her glasses away, puts on a small hat, gets up and walks to the left; camera follows as she passes three windows, stops at her last small window, pours herself another drink from a bottle in the cabinet and downs it quickly. Upright and ready, she leaves her apartment. Camera follows her as she goes through the door and down the corridor. *[Long-duration silent pantomime, without interruption.]* (44 sec.)
378. Cut to same medium close-up of Jefferies as he finishes looking

through his lens, puts it away and looks up. (4 sec.)
379. Cut to long shot of the musician's studio, where he plays the piano. Two young women, dressed for a party, come in. (8 sec.)
380. Cut back to same medium close-up of Jefferies, who changes the direction of his gaze. (3 sec.)
381. Cut to quick pan in long shot of the dancer's window. A full rehearsal is taking place. The dancer leaps into the arms of a male dancer. A woman, who seems to be directing, sits on the left. Camera pans to the left revealing the alleyway. Miss Lonelyhearts is seen entering the frame; she hesitates and stops at a lamppost. (15 sec.)
382. Cut back to same medium close-up of Jefferies, who lifts his camera to his eye. (5 sec.)
383. Cut to medium close-up of Miss Lonelyhearts, her back to the camera, as she starts crossing the street (away from camera). She enters the restaurant across and sits at a near table; a waiter approaches to take her order. As she starts ordering, we see the bulk of Thorwald on the street outside the restaurant, as he comes back toward home. He is dressed in a blue jacket, straw hat and tie. For a moment he obliterates her image (in the background). As he is about to step down the sidewalk to cross, a taxi passes, missing him by inches. Thorwald steps back, startled; furious, he resumes crossing and leaves the frame. (30 sec.)
384. Cut back to same medium close-up of Jefferies, animated; he adjusts his lens, puts it away, rolls his wheelchair back into the shade, then picks up his lens again (in medium shot). (10 sec.)
385. Cut to medium shot of Thorwald's corridor as he walks toward his door, opens it, enters the apartment and walks to the right. Camera pans with him, passing three windows. He carries a box of laundry from the cleaner's; he puts it on the unmade bed, takes the shirts out and adds more shirts from the drawer. (29 sec.)
386. Cut back to same medium shot of Jefferies; he puts away the camera, starts dialing the phone (which is outside the frame). He finally reaches the detective's home and leaves a message for him to come over right away. (45 sec.)
387. Cut to medium shot of Thorwald by the bedroom window, holding his wife's bag. He walks over to the living room. Camera

follows him; he sits down in the big chair and starts dialing, obviously a long-distance number. (13 sec.)
388. Cut back to same medium shot of Jefferies with his lens on the ready. (1 sec.)
389. Cut back to same medium shot of Thorwald (via telephoto), on the phone while handling his wife's jewelry. He seems to be in good spirits. (14 sec.)
390. Cut back to same shot of Jefferies, looking through the lens. Jefferies: "Long distance again." (1 sec.)
391. Cut back to tighter medium shot of Thorwald still on the phone, with more concentration, while holding in his hand a ring, then another, which he puts away on a side table. (19 sec.)
392. Cut back to the same medium shot of Jefferies; he puts his camera away and tries to listen; however, the noise of a party obliterates Thorwald's voice. (15 sec.)
393. Cut to long shot of the musician's studio, from where the noise is coming. The party is in full swing. New guests of every description and social status are filing in. (8 sec.)
394. Cut back to same shot of Jefferies. He is upset—he saw something and puts his lens to view. (5 sec.)
395. Cut to medium shot of Thorwald as he gets off his chair and walks over to the bedroom, puts away the empty purse and looks around. (10 sec.)
396. Cut to wider medium shot of Jefferies as his door opens and Lisa enters with a new hat and outfit and with an elegant attaché case. Jefferies: "What did you do with your hair?" Lisa: "Well, I just. . . . " Jefferies: "Say take a look at Thorwald! He's getting ready to pull out for good. Look at him." (11 sec.)
397. Cut to long shot of the two windows. Thorwald is in the living room. (5 sec.)
398. Cut to medium long shot of Lisa and Jefferies. Lisa walks over to the other side of his chair. Lisa: "Doesn't seem to be in any hurry." Jefferies: "Aw, he's been laying all his things out on one of the beds. Shirts, suits, coats, socks—even his wife's—that alligator handbag his wife had on the bedpost." Lisa: "What about it?" Jefferies: "He had it hidden in the dresser. At least it was there. He took it out, went to

the telephone to make a long-distance call. He had his wife's jewelry in the handbag. He seemed worried about it—asked somebody's advice over the telephone." Lisa: "Someone not his wife?" Jefferies: "Yeah—well, I never saw him ask her for advice. She volunteered plenty, but I never saw him ask her for any." (33 sec.)
399. Cut back to long shot of Thorwald's windows; he walks over toward the door, turns off the lights and exits to the corridor. (10 sec.)
400. Cut back to medium long two-shot of Jefferies and Lisa, who walks over to the left as camera follows. She is about to put on the lights, but stops. (12 sec.)
401. Cut to medium shot of Jefferies. He checks with his long lens if it's safe to put on the lights. (5 sec.)
402. Cut to medium shot of Lisa by the lamp, waiting. (1 sec.)
403. Cut back to same medium shot of Jefferies with lens; he says: "OK, turn it on now." (4 sec.)
404. Cut back to same medium shot of Lisa; she turns the light on and walks to the other lamp: "All day long I've been trying to keep my mind on my work." Jefferies: "Thinking about Thorwald?" Camera follows her, she turns lamp on: "And you, and your friend, Doyle. Did you hear from him again, since he left?" Jefferies: "Not a word. He said he was going over to check the railroad station and the trunk." "Must still be at it." She walks over to the third lamp, puts it on, walks closer to Jefferies to a medium two-shot. Jefferies: "Somethin' on your mind?" Lisa: "It doesn't make sense to me." Jefferies: "What doesn't? Lisa: "Women aren't that unpredictable." Jefferies: "Umm. Well, I can't guess what you're thinking." Lisa: "A woman has a favorite handbag—and it always hangs on her bedpost where she can get at it easily. And then all of a sudden she goes away on a trip and leaves it behind. Why?" Jefferies: "Because she didn't know she was going on a trip. And where she's going she wouldn't need the handbag." Lisa: "Yes, but only her husband would know that. And that jewelry. Women don't keep their jewelry in a purse, getting all twisted and scratched and tangled up." Jefferies: "Well, do they hide in it their husbands' clothes?" Lisa: "They do not. And they don't leave it behind, either. Why, a woman going anywhere

but the hospital would always take makeup, perfume and jewelry." Jefferies: "Put that over there. That's inside stuff, huh?" Lisa: "That's basic equipment. And you don't leave it behind in your husband's drawer in your favorite handbag." Jefferies: "Well, I'm with you, sweetie—I'm with you. Tom Doyle has a pat answer for that, though." Lisa: "That Mrs. Thorwald left at 6 a.m. yesterday with her husband?" Jefferies: "According to those witnesses." (1 min., 24 sec.)
405. Cut on action to medium close-up of Lisa as she takes off her stylish hat: Lisa: "Well, I have a pat rebuttal for Mr. Doyle. That couldn't have been Mrs. Thorwald." Jefferies: "Oh?" Lisa: "Or I don't know women." (3 sec.)
406. Cut to high medium close-up of Jefferies: "What about the witnesses?" (3 sec.)
407. Cut to same medium close-up of Lisa: "I agree, they saw a woman, but it was not Mrs. Thorwald. That is, not yet." (11 sec.)
408. Cut back to same shot of Jefferies: "Is that so?" (1 sec.)
409. Cut back to same medium close-up of Lisa, smiling. (2 sec.)
410. Cut to same shot of Jefferies: "Come here." She turns around and sits in his lap; camera adjusts gently and moves in, into a medium close-up of the two, profile-to-profile. They kiss, and converse. Lisa: "I'd like to see your friend's face when we tell him. He doesn't sound like much of a detective." Jefferies: "Oh, hun, don't be too hard on him. He's a steady worker. I sure wish he'd show up." Lisa: "Mmmm. Don't rush him. We have all night." Jefferies: "We have all what?" Lisa: "Night. I'm going to stay with you." She kisses him. Jefferies: "Well, you'll have to clear that with my landlord." Lisa: "I have the whole weekend off." Jefferies: "Well, that's very nice, but I just have one bed." Lisa: "If you say something else I'll stay tomorrow night, too." Jefferies: "I won't be able to give you any pajamas." She walks out of the embrace. (55 sec.)
411. Cut to medium shot of Lisa, who walks to the back of the room, picks up the attaché case and comes back to him, sits down on his lap again and shows him how her bag doubles as a suitcase, with nightgown, slippers and accessories: Lisa: "You said I'll have to live out of one suitcase. I'll bet yours isn't this small." Jefferies: "This is a suitcase?" Lisa: "Well, a Mark Cross overnight case, anyway. Com-

pact, but simple enough." Jefferies: "Looks like you packed in a hurry. Look at this. Isn't that amazing?" Lisa: "I'll trade you...my feminine intuition for a bed for the night." Jefferies: "I'll go along with that." Lisa: "There's that song again." She then puts it away on the table and comes closer to Jefferies; then she again hears the tune she kept hearing before. Camera moves in into medium close-up of Lisa as she listens. (44 sec.)
412. Cut to long shot of the musician's studio, crowded with guests; the music emanates from there. (7 sec.)
413. Cut to medium two-shot of Jefferies and Lisa, who asks: "How does a man get an inspiration for a song like that?" Jefferies retorts ironically: "He gets it from his landlady every month." Lisa: "It's utterly beautiful. I wish I could be creative." Jefferies: "Well, sweetie, you are. You have a great talent for creating difficult situations." Lisa: "I do?" Jefferies: "Sure. Like staying here all night, uninvited." Lisa: "Surprise is the most important element of attack. And besides, you're not up on your private eye literature. When they're in trouble, it's always their girl Friday who gets them out of it." Jefferies: "Is she the girl that saves him from the clutches of the seductive showgirls and the overpassionate daughters of the rich?" Lisa: "The same." Jefferies: "That's the one, huh? It's funny—he never ends up marrying her. . . . " Lisa lies down on the couch by the window, listening. (47 sec.)
414. Cut to medium close-up of Lisa, reclining. Then she gets up, walks over (camera follows her): "I'll change into something more comfortable . . . I'll make some coffee . . . . " She disappears in the back. Jefferies: "With some brandy," adds Jefferies (off screen). (18 sec.)
415. Cut to medium long shot of the newlywed's small window. The man in a tank top shirt and white shorts pulls up the shade; he leans out of the window, puffing a cigarette. In the background, we again hear his wife calling him back. "Ha-a-a-r-r-ry!" (9 sec.)
416. Cut to medium shot of Jefferies, reacting. In the back his door opens, and his friend Doyle enters: "Jeff." He puts his hat away. (12 sec.)
417. Cut to medium shot of Jefferies, turning: "Hi." (1 sec.)
418. Cut back to medium shot of Doyle, who hears Lisa singing in

the kitchen (her shadow is on the ceiling). (6 sec.)
419. Cut back to medium shot of Jefferies, slightly embarrassed. (4 sec.)
420. Cut back to same medium shot of Doyle. He notices the woman's accessories. (5 sec.)
421. Cut to close-up of Lisa's open attaché case with her nightgown. (2 sec.)
422. Cut to same medium shot of Jefferies, getting apprehensive. (2 sec.)
423. Cut back to same medium shot of Doyle. He lights a cigarette, walks over to the window in medium close-up and looks out (music is loud). (13 sec.)
424. Cut back to long shot of the musician's studio. The party is peaking, crowded. (3 sec.)
425. Cut to long shot of Thorwald's dark windows. (3 sec.)
426. Cut to medium shot profile of Doyle (2 sec.)
427. Cut to high medium shot of Jefferies slowly moving his chair. (4 sec.)
428. Cut back to same profile shot of Doyle; he turns, then moves back. The back of Jefferies' head appears in the foreground (unexpectedly, he wheels in). Doyle: "What else have you got on this man Thorwald?" Jefferies: "Enough to scare me you wouldn't show up in time, and we'd lose him." Doyle: "You think he's getting out of here?" (10 sec.)
429. Reverse over-the-shoulder medium shot toward Jefferies; he tells him what he saw: "He got everything he owns laid out there...waiting to be packed." (4 sec.)
430. Cut to medium close-up of the detective, listening. (2 sec.)
431. Cut to medium shot of Lisa entering from the kitchen, two drinks in her hands; she walks into a medium close-up, puts the drinks down. Lisa: "I'm just warming some brandy. Mr Doyle, I presume?" (4 sec.)
432. Cut back to same medium close-up of the detective. Jefferies (off screen): "Tom, this is Miss Lisa Freemont." (2 sec.)
433. Cut back to same medium close-up of Lisa, who offers a drink to the detective. (2 sec.)

434. Cut back to same medium close up of the detective; a glass of brandy enters his frame. He mumbles: "How do you do?" (4 sec.)
435. Cut back to same shot of Lisa, as she walks back, starting to say: "We think Thorwald's guilty." (2 sec.)
436. Cut back to same shot of the detective, who looks down. (2 sec.)
437. Cut to close-up insert of Lisa's bag with the nightgown. (2 sec.)
438. Cut to medium close of Jefferies, reacting. (1 sec.)
439. Cut back to same shot of the detective; subtle play of eye contact. (1 sec.)
440. Cut back to same shot of Jefferies, who mumbles to the detective: "Be careful." We hear the phone ring. Jefferies picks it up—it's for the detective—and hands over the phone. (12 sec.)
441. Cut on action to a wider two-shot as the detective picks up the receiver, talks very briefly and then hangs it up. Lisa enters the frame with her drink. "The coffee'll be ready soon. Jeff, aren't you going to tell him about the jewelry?" Doyle: "Jewelry?" Jefferies: "He's got his wife's jewelry hidden in his clothes in the bedroom over there." Doyle: "You sure it belonged to his wife?" Lisa: "It was in her favorite handbag. And Mr. Doyle, that can only lead to one conclusion." Doyle: "Namely?" Jefferies: "That it was not Mrs. Thorwald that left with him yesterday morning." Doyle: "You figured that out, eh?" Jefferies: "I did." Lisa: "Well, it's simply that women don't leave their jewelry behind when they go on a trip." Jefferies: "Come on, come on, Tom—now you don't really need any of this information, do you?" The detective downs his drink, walks away to pick up his hat. Camera moves into close-up of the detective, who says: "Thorwald is no more a murderer than I am." (1 min., 4 sec.)
442. Cut to a medium two-shot of Lisa and Jefferies, who says: "You mean, you can explain everything what's going on over there?" (6 sec.)
443. Cut to medium shot of the detective in three-quarter profile. He answers: "No, neither can you . . . . There's a private world out there. People do in private lots of things they cannot possibly explain in public." He comes forward to a tighter medium shot. (10 sec.)

444. Cut back to same two-shot of Lisa and Jefferies: Lisa: "Like disposing of their wives." (3 sec.)
445. Cut back to same medium shot of the detective: "Get that idea out of your mind, it can only lead in the wrong direction." (6 sec.)
446. Cut back to the same two-shot of Lisa and Jefferies, who says: "What about the knife and the saw?" (2 sec.)
447. Cut back to same shot of the detective: "You own a saw?" (1 sec.)
448. Cut back to same shot of Lisa and Jefferies, who hesitates: "Well, at home . . . in the garage." (6 sec.)
449. Cut back to same medium shot of the detective, who shoots: "And a couple hundred knives you owned in your lifetime." He turns away to leave, adding: "Your logic is backward." (6 sec.)
450. Cut to Lisa moving to him; camera follows to a wide two-shot. Lisa: "You can't ignore the wife disappearing, and the trunk and the jewelry!" Doyle: "I checked the railroad station. He bought a ticket. Ten minutes later he put his wife on the train. Destination: Merritsville. The witnesses are that deep." Lisa: "That might have been a woman, but it couldn't have been Mrs. Thorwald. That jewelry . . . . " Doyle: "Look, Miss Freemont—that feminine intuition stuff—it sells magazines, but in real life, it's still a fairy tale. I don't know how many wasted years I've spent tracking down leads based on female intuition." Jefferies: "All right!" (29 sec.)
451. Cut to medium shot of Jefferies, wheeling himself toward the two into a wide three-shot (medium long shot). Jefferies: "I take it you didn't find the trunk, and all this is from an old speech you once made at the Policeman's Ball." Doyle: "I found the trunk—a half hour after I left here." Lisa: "I suppose it's normal for a man to tie up a trunk with heavy rope." Doyle: "Well, if the lock is broken, yes." Jefferies: "What did you find inside the trunk? A surly note to me?" Doyle: "Mrs. Thorwald's clothes—clean, well-packed—not stylish, but presentable." Lisa: "Didn't you take them off to the crime lab?" Doyle: "I sent them on their merry and legal way." *[Separation is thus resolved.]* Detective sits down into a soft chair, breaking the three-shot into a two-shot of detective and Jefferies, who says: "Why would a woman who's taking a simple short trip—does she take everything

she owns?" Doyle: "Let's let the female psychology department handle that one, huh?" Lisa: "I would say it looked as if she wasn't coming back." Lisa enters frame, back to a three-shot. Doyle: "That's what's known as a family problem." Jefferies: "And if she wasn't coming back, why didn't he tell his landlord? I'll tell you why he didn't tell his landlord, because he was hiding something." (48 sec.)
452. Cut to tight medium over-the-shoulder shot from Jefferies toward the detective, who looks to his left. (1 sec.)
453. Cut to close-up of the insert of Lisa's attaché case with nightgown hanging out. (2 sec.)
454. Cut back to same over-the-shoulder shot toward the detective who asks: "Do you tell everything to the landlord?" (4 sec.)
455. Cut to a reverse over-the-shoulder shot toward Jefferies: "I told you to be careful Tom." Jefferies wheels away from the windows. Camera follows. (12 sec.)
456. Cut to wide two-shot of the detective on the left and Lisa standing on the right. Detective leans back, and says: "What about forgetting all that, relax with a friendly drink and tell each other lies about the war and the good old days." Lisa: "You mean you're through with the case?" Detective: "There's no case to be through with. . . . Miss Freemont, how about that drink?" Lisa moves to where Jefferies is, camera follows into a long two-shot of Jefferies in the chair and Lisa standing next to him, forlorn. (28 sec.)
457. Cut to frontal medium shot of Doyle, who, after a pause, says: "Well. . . I guess I better go home, get some sleep." He gets up, downs his drink, spills some on his jacket. (18 sec.)
458. Cut to closer medium shot of Lisa and Jefferies, who turns away to the window. (2 sec.)
459. Cut back to same shot of the detective as he moves on, picking up his things; he snaps, ironically: "Oh, if you need further help, follow the yellow pages in your telephone directory." (9 sec.)
460. Cut to same two-shot of Lisa and Jefferies. Lisa, on the side: "This is the exit line." Jefferies turns and asks: "Who was the trunk addressed to?" (6 sec.)
461. Cut to medium long shot of Doyle: "To Mrs. Anna Thorwald." (2 sec.)

462. Cut back to two-shot of Lisa and Jefferies, who asks: "So, we have to wait to find out who picked it up?" (2 sec.)
463. Cut back to same shot of Doyle: "The telephone call I had, I gave him your number; I hope you don't mind." (6 sec.)
464. Cut back to same two-shot of Lisa and Jefferies, who asks: "Who from?" (1 sec.)
465. Cut back to shot of the detective: "The police department in Connecticut. The trunk was picked up by Mrs. Thorwald." He leaves, followed by his shadow on the door. (10 sec.)
466. Cut back to a more-frontal medium two-shot of Lisa and Jefferies, who is looking out. The door is heard shutting. (4 sec.)
467. Cut to long shot of the musician's studio. The party is still going strong, with people singing, kissing. (4 sec.)
468. Cut back to same medium shot of Lisa and Jefferies scanning the windows. (5 sec.)
469. Cut to long shot of the dancer's window. She exercises her legs in her bed. (3 sec.)
470. Cut back to same medium two-shot of Jefferies and Lisa, who leans over and directs Jefferies to look down. (2 sec.)
471. Cut to long shot of Miss Lonelyhearts' windows. She is seen in the corridor coming back with a man. Lonelyhearts puts the lights on, they enter the dining room and she follows him to the table. (12 sec.)
472. Cut back to two-shot of Jefferies and Lisa; they look. (2 sec.)
473. Cut to tighter medium long shot of Lonelyhearts' dining-room window. *[Note: This is the first time we get a closer shot of the windows without the help of such devices as the field glasses or the telephoto lens.]* Lonelyhearts picks up a bottle of wine. (6 sec.)
474. Cut back to same two-shot of Lisa and Jefferies. They wonder and look. (2 sec.)
475. Cut back to same medium long shot of the window. Lonelyhearts is pouring wine, they cheer each other and drink (in profile). The man reaches to her for a kiss. (17 sec.)
476. Cut back to same two-shot of Lisa and Jefferies; he looks disapprovingly, she wonders. (4 sec.)
477. Cut back to same medium long shot of Lonelyhearts' window.

She breaks away from him, pointing to the open window. She walks over and lowers the venetian blinds. However, we can still see through as the man grabs her and forces her down—a struggle ensues. They get up, Lonelyhearts strikes him on the face. (25 sec.)
478. Cut back to same two-shot of Lisa and Jefferies, who are embarrassed. (2 sec.)
479. Cut back to same shot of the window. The man backs up toward the door. Camera pans as they both reach the small window by the door; he walks out, and she shuts the door and starts crying. The man leaves down the corridor. Lonelyhearts goes back to the dining room (as camera pans with her). She sits down, crying. (26 sec.)
480. Cut back to same medium two-shot of Jefferies and Lisa. (3 sec.)
481. Cut on action to a reverse shot crossing the axis. Lisa is screen right then moves to the left, camera follows, leaving Jefferies out of frame. Lisa, in long shot, reaches fireplace as we hear Jefferies off screen: "I wonder if it is ethical to watch other people with binoculars and long-focus lenses." (18 sec.)
482. Cut to medium close-up of Jefferies, in profile, as he continues: "You suppose it is ethical even if he did not commit a crime?" (7 sec.)
483. Cut to same long shot of Lisa at the fireplace. She replies (without turning): "I'm not much on rear-window ethics." (4 sec.)
484. Cut back to same medium close-up of Jefferies, in profile: "Of course they can do the same thing to me, watch me, like a bug under glass if they want to." (9 sec.)
485. Cut back to same long shot of Lisa. *[A longer dramatic scene with floating camera follows for a minute.]* She turns to camera and moves across the room toward Jefferies. She expresses distress at their bad humor: "Jeff, you know if someone came in here, they wouldn't believe what they see?" "What?" "You and me with long faces—plunged into despair, because we find out a man didn't kill his wife. We're two of the most frightening ghouls I've ever known. You'd think we could be a little bit happy that the poor woman is alive and well." She kisses him on the neck, camera moves in to medium close-up of the two. Then Lisa starts lowering their blinds one by

one, camera follows her from left to right. Lisa picks up her night things and walks across to change, saying: "A preview of coming attractions." In long shot at the bathroom door, she turns to Jefferies and asks: "Did Mr. Doyle think I stole this case?" (1 min., 2 sec.)
486. Cut to long shot of Jefferies (full chair and cast): "No, Lisa, I don't think he did." (3 sec.)
487. Cut back to same long shot of Lisa as she elegantly enters the bathroom. *FADE-OUT.* (8 sec.)
488. *FADE-IN* (shortly after) to a medium shot of Jefferies, finishing a glass of brandy. (7 sec.)
489. Cut to long shot of Lisa emerging from the bathroom door—displaying her gorgeous white nightgown: "What do you think?" She floats through the room toward Jefferies in a display of fashion, into a long shot of the two. (Some lights and outlines of the wall across can be seen through the blinds.) "I'll rephrase the question." Jefferies: "Thank you." Lisa: "Do you like it?" Jefferies: "Yes, I like it." Lisa: "Well. . . . " Suddenly, a loud shriek and a female scream are heard from outside. Lisa quickly rolls up the middle blind and we can see Lisa and Jefferies, their backs to the camera, watching the female dog owner on the fire escape, lamenting in despair. (22 sec.)
490. Cut to closer medium long shot of the same woman, her husband joins her and they both look down. (7 sec.)
491. Cut to wide medium shot (frontal) of Lisa and Jefferies, looking. (2 sec.)
492. Cut to high long shot of the garden. The familiar little dog, now lifeless, is lying on the concrete. (2 sec.)
493. Cut to long shot of the musician's studio; people at the party have noticed the disturbance. (1 sec.)
494. Cut to medium long shot of the newlyweds' small window. They lift the window and lean out, looking. (1 sec.)
495. Cut to long shot of the dancer's balcony; she comes out. (3 sec.)
496. Cut to high long shot of the garden area; the sculptress and Lonelyhearts emerge. (2 sec.)
497. Cut back to long shot of the little dog on the cement. (1 sec.)
498. Cut to low long shot of the balcony; Lonelyhearts is coming down. (1 sec.)

499. Cut to same shot of the musician's studio, people looking. (3 sec.)
500. Cut back to high long shot of the garden. Lonelyhearts is picking up the dog, crying: "He is dead, his neck is broken." (4 sec.)
501. Cut to full long shot, the widest and longest so far: Two sides of the wall with windows are in view, people are coming out into the garden and onto fire escapes. The owner of the dead dog shouts: "Which one, which one of you, did it to him?" (6 sec.)
502. Cut to medium long shot of balcony with couple. (2 sec.)
503. Cut to low medium long shot of the fire escape with woman lamenting. (3 sec.)
504. Cut to long shot of the musician's studio with people filing out. (2 sec.)
505. Cut back to fire escape, where the woman is loudly accusing "the guilty killer." (4 sec.)
506. Cut back to high long shot of the garden. Lonelyhearts is putting the dog into the basket. (4 sec.)
507. Cut back to fire escape as the man starts pulling up the rope. (1 sec.)
508. Cut back to same shot of the garden; the basket starts going up, Lonelyhearts stands by. (1 sec.)
509. Cut back to newlyweds' small window; they look on. (2 sec.)
510. Cut back to same shot of the fire escape; the dog is being pulled up; woman is still wailing. (5 sec.)
511. Cut to low medium close-up of the dancer, standing by the fire escape [*The first time we see her that close and outside her room*]. (1 sec.)
512. Cut back to couple on the fire escape. The dog comes up in the basket; the woman cries. (6 sec.)
513. Cut to closer medium shot of Lisa and Jefferies, looking. (2 sec.)
514. Cut back to same shot of the fire escape as the man takes out the dead dog and hands it to his wife, who breaks down and turns away. (4 sec.)
515. Cut to high medium close-up of Lonelyhearts, looking up [*The closest shot of her so far*]. (2 sec.)
516. Cut back to same shot of the fire escape with the couple hold-

ing the dog. The woman again accuses her neighbors. (4 sec.)
517. Cut to same two-shot of Lisa and Jefferies, looking. (1 sec.)
518. Cut back to same shot of the fire escape with the dog. The woman runs back to the apartment; the husband, with the dog, follows her. (8 sec.)
519. Cut back to same shot of the musician's studio. The people at the party seem to be moving back inside. (3 sec.)
520. Cut back to the same shot of the newlyweds, who are also retreating inside. (3 sec.)
521. Cut to same shot of the balcony, where the couple is reentering their apartment. (3 sec.)
522. Cut to same shot of the dancer, now returning to her room. (2 sec.)
523. Cut to the sculptor reentering her apartment. (3 sec.)
524. Cut back to same shot of Lisa and Jefferies, who says: "I was almost convinced by Tom Doyle that I was wrong." Camera moves into a tighter medium two-shot. Jefferies continues: "Look, the only person who did not come out . . . " (31 sec.)
525. Cut to medium long shot of Thorwald's dark windows; faint glow of a cigarette light can be discerned. (4 sec.)
526. Cut back to same medium close-up of Jefferies and Lisa, who adds: "Why would one want to kill a little dog? . . . Because he knew too much." (4 sec.)
527. Cut back to same shot of Thorwald's windows, the flicker of the cigarette light is still there. (10 sec.)
FADE-OUT.
528. *FADE-IN.* Next day, interior of Jefferies' apartment from the back. A long shot of the three, Jefferies (on the left), Lisa and nurse Stella (on the right), their backs are to the camera, and they look out the window. (4 sec.)
529. Cut to reverse (with crossing of the axis), the same group facing the camera. Jefferies, now on the right: "You think this was worth waiting to see?" He has the long lens up. (4 sec.)
530. Cut to medium shot of a small window in Thorwald's bathroom. Thorwald, partially observed, is wiping off (or washing) the wall above the bathtub. (2 sec.)

531. Cut back to same three-shot (as in shot no. 528); they watch. (3 sec.)
532. Cut to medium shot of Lisa and the nurse, looking. Stella: "The blood must have been splattered on the wall; that's why Thorwald cleans it." Lisa is visibly discomfited: "Stella, your choice of words." (13 sec.)
533. Cut to close-up of Jefferies, looking without camera. (1 sec.)
534. Cut to high long shot of the garden. (1 sec.)
535. Cut back to same close-up of Jefferies, looking intensely; he turns to Lisa: "Lisa, there's a small yellow box on the shelf; would you give it to me?" (5 sec.)
536. Cut back to wide three-shot (as in no. 526). Lisa is getting the box. Jefferies: "Hand me the viewer"—we see him inserting a slide into the viewer—"I took it a few weeks ago"; he adds: "I think I solved the murder," as he starts looking at the slide. (23 sec.)
537. Cut to medium close-up of Lisa and Jefferies as he keeps looking through the viewer: "I think I know why Thorwald killed the dog." He hands the viewer to Lisa. (13 sec.)
538. Cut to picture of the slide, showing the part of the garden by the rosebushes. Jefferies' voice: "What do you see?" The slide turns dark and back to light again. (7 sec.)
539. Cut back to same shot of the three, again in long shot. Lisa says she saw the flower bed. Jefferies: "But there is a small difference; look at the flowers, Thorwald's pet flowers." (16 sec.)
540. Cut to close-up of Stella as she is handed the viewer. Again, we see dark and light slides. Jefferies, off screen: "The zinnias got shorter in two weeks." (10 sec.)
541. Cut back to same three-shot. They discuss the alternatives. Lisa and Jefferies think the flowers were replaced. Stella: "There's something buried there." Lisa: "Mrs. Thorwald!" Stella: "You haven't spent much time around cemeteries, have you? Mr. Thorwald could scarcely put his wife's body in a plot of ground about one foot square. Unless of course, he put her in standing on end and then he wouldn't need a knife and saw. No, my idea is she's scattered all over town. A leg in the East River. . . . " Lisa: "Oh, Stella, please!" Jefferies: "No, no, no, there's something in there. Those flowers have been taken

out and put back in." Lisa: "Maybe it's the knife and the saw." Jefferies: "Yeah, could be." Stella: "Call Lieutenant Doyle!" Lisa: "No, let's wait. Let's wait till it gets a little darker—and I'll go over there and dig them up." Jefferies: "You'll go . . . ? You won't dig anything up and get your neck broken. No, no—I'm not gonna call Doyle until I can produce Mrs. Thorwald's body; and what we've got to do is find a way to get into that apartment." They notice something across. Stella: "He's packing!" (52 sec.)
542. Cut to long shot of Thorwald's windows; he is in the bedroom packing. (3 sec.)
543. Cut back to same three-shot. Jefferies, whose back is to the camera, starts to wheel himself around. He asks for a piece of paper and starts scribbling something. (12 sec.)
544. Cut to new very high long shot of the three. Jefferies, in the center, keeps writing in block letters. Camera starts moving in on the note to a close-up. It reads: "What have you done with her?" He folds it and puts it in an envelope, addressing it to Lars Thorwald. Before he finishes: *FADE-OUT.* (29 sec.)
545. *FADE-IN.* A brief deletion, then cut to a long shot of Jefferies and the nurse, standing by the window, their backs to the camera. Jefferies has long lens by his eye. (2 sec.)
546. Cut to medium shot (via telephoto) of the alleyway; Lisa enters frame, letter in hand; she waves toward Jefferies and goes out to the right. (5 sec.)
547. Cut back to same two-shot from the back of nurse; Jefferies still has his camera at the eye. (4 sec.)
548. Cut to reverse view (crossing the axis) of the above two-shot; Jefferies still has camera up, then takes it away from his eye. (3 sec.)
549. Cut to a long shot of Thorwald's three windows. He is in the bedroom lighting a cigar. At the same time, in his window by the corridor, we see Lisa tiptoeing to his door and gently pushing the envelope under. Thorwald apparently hears the noise and walks over. Lisa hurries out down the corridor and disappears just as Thorwald's bulk comes through the door to look. He picks up the letter. (24 sec.)
550. Cut back to same two-shot of nurse and Jefferies, who is in-

tensely looking through his long lens. (2 sec.)
551. Cut to medium close-up (via the lens) of Thorwald opening and reading the note, getting tense. (6 sec.)
552. Cut back to same two-shot of Jefferies, looking through the telephoto lens. (1 sec.)
553. Cut back to same medium close-up of Thorwald as he turns to his door. (1 sec.)
554. Cut back to same two-shot; Jefferies takes the camera down and says: "We did it." (1 sec.)
555. Cut to long shot of Thorwald's windows. We see him running down his corridor. (1 sec.)
556. Cut back to same two-shot of nurse and Jefferies. They both worry about Lisa. Jefferies exclaims: "He's coming!" (3 sec.)
557. Cut to same long shot of the wall with windows across. Lisa emerges from the ground level door behind by the wall; upstairs, Thorwald walks back toward his door. (11 sec.)
558. Cut back to same two-shot. Nurse holds onto Jefferies. (2 sec.)
559. Cut back to same long shot of the windows across. Thorwald walks out onto the fire escape, looking up, while Lisa, downstairs, jumps into the corridor and runs toward the street exit. (3 sec.)
560. Cut back to same two-shot. Nurse and Jefferies are somewhat relieved. Nurse: "Thank heavens that's over." (5 sec.)
561. Cut to closer medium long shot of Thorwald's. He is walking past two windows, letter in hand, worried; camera pans with him. (4 sec.)
562. Cut back to same two-shot. Nurse goes to get a drink. (3 sec.)
563. Cut back to long shot of Thorwald's. He returns to his packing in the bedroom, and is tense. (10 sec.)
564. Cut back to same two-shot. Jefferies: "A-ha? He's leaving." Nurse: "When?" Jefferies hands her the camera. (8 sec.)
565. Cut to medium close-up of the nurse looking through the lens. (2 sec.)
566. Cut to medium shot (via telephoto) of Lonelyhearts' window. She's handling a bottle of pills, places some on the table, walks over to the kitchen (as camera follows her), gets some water in a glass and returns to the dining room. Off screen the nurse voices her concern.

(19 sec.)
567. Cut back to same two-shot. The nurse continues to look through the camera. (2 sec.)
568. Cut back to same medium shot of Lonelyhearts, who picks up a book, most likely the Bible (it has a big cross on the cover), and sits down. (2 sec.)
569. Cut to wide long shot of Jefferies' room as Lisa enters through the door. (1 sec.)
570. Cut to medium close-up of Lisa's face; she excitedly asks: "What was his reaction? . . . I mean, when he read the note?" (4 sec.)
571. Cut to close-up of Jefferies' face looking up to her in admiration for what she had done. The nurse (off screen): "Well, it wasn't the kind of expression that would get him a quick loan at the bank." (4 sec.)
572. Cut to full three-shot (long shot). Lisa comes closer, she looks out: "He has the handbag." Jefferies grabs the camera. (6 sec.)
573. Cut to medium close-up of Thorwald in the bedroom (via telephoto) as he takes things from the handbag; he thinks, and finally walks in the direction of the next room yet never reaches it; he is behind the wall space between the windows. He comes back to the bedroom and throws the bag into his valise. (16 sec.)
574. Cut back to same long shot (three-shot), with Lisa on the left in the foreground. Jefferies puts away the camera and says: "Suppose Mrs. Thorwald's wedding ring is among the jewelry he has in that handbag? Now, during the phone conversation he held up three rings—one with a diamond, one with a big stone of some sort and then just a plain gold band." Lisa: "And the last thing she would leave behind would be her wedding ring. Stella, do you ever leave yours at home?" The nurse: "The only way anybody would get that ring would be to chop off my finger! Let's go down and find out what's buried in the garden." Lisa: "Why not? I've always wanted to meet Mrs. Thorwald." Jefferies: "What are you two talking about?" The nurse: "You got a shovel?" Jefferies: "A shovel? Of course, I don't have a shovel." The nurse: "There's probably one in the basement." Jefferies: "Now wait—hold on a minute." Lisa: "Jeff, if you're squeamish, just don't look." Jefferies: "Squeamish—I'm not squea-

mish! I just don't want you two to end up like that dog ended up, that's all." The nurse: "Oh. You know, Miss Freemont—he might just have something there?" Jefferies: "Now, there's no sense in taking any chances or anything. Here, give me the phone book." She returns. Lisa hands directory to Jeff. Lisa: "What for?" Jefferies: "Maybe I can get him out of that apartment." The nurse: "We only need a few minutes." Lisa: "How?" Jefferies: "Chelsea 2-7099—2-7099. We scared him once—maybe we can scare him again. Well, I guess I'm using that word "we" a little freely. You're taking all the chances." (1 min., 33 sec.)
575. Cut to medium long shot of Lonelyhearts' window. She is lowering the blind and sits down, depressed. (5 sec.)
576. Cut back to same long three-shot. Jefferies wheels himself back, in order not to be seen, and starts dialing a number. The nurse and Lisa are looking out at Thorwald (14 sec.)
577. Cut to long shot of Thorwald's windows. In the bedroom, Thorwald reacts to the ringing, and walks over to the dining room, looks at the phone, hesitates. (13 sec.)
578. Cut to medium close-up of Jefferies, holding his receiver, waiting and murmuring: "Go ahead, pick it up." (2 sec.)
579. Cut to long shot of the dining-room window. Thorwald still hesitates. Off screen, Jefferies' voice encourages him to pick it up: "You wonder if it's your girlfriend?" (8 sec.)
580. Cut back to same medium close-up of Jefferies, repeating: "Pick it up." (1 sec.)
581. Cut back to same long shot of Thorwald as he picks up the phone. (1 sec.)
582. Cut back to same medium close-up of Jefferies, who eagerly puts the receiver to his ear. (1 sec.)
583. Cut back to same shot of Thorwald, who hesitates then finally says: "Hello." (2 sec.)
584. Cut back to same shot of Jefferies: "Did you get my note?" Long pause. (5 sec.)
585. Cut back to same long shot of Thorwald, who stands frozen. Jefferies, off screen, asks: "Did you get it?" (5 sec.)
586. Cut back to new medium shot of the nurse and Lisa, listening.

Thorwald's voice over the phone asks: "Who are you?" Jefferies replies off screen: "I'll give you a chance to find out." (3 sec.)
587. Cut to same shot of Thorwald still on the phone. Jefferies' voice, via receiver: "Meet me at the bar of the Albert Hotel right away!" (2 sec.)
588. Cut back to same medium close-up of Jefferies. Thorwald's voice is heard over the receiver: "Why should I?" Jefferies: "A little business meeting." (5 sec.)
589. Cut to same shot of Thorwald, listening. (3 sec.)
590. Cut back to two-shot of Lisa and the nurse, listening. Jefferies' voice off screen: "To settle the estate of your late wife." Thorwald's voice: "I don't know what you mean." (4 sec.)
591. Cut back to same medium close-up of Jefferies, resolutely: "Come on, quit stallin', Thorwald, or I'll hang up and call the police." Thorwald's voice: "I only have a hundred dollars or so." (4 sec.)
592. Cut back to same long shot of Thorwald, still on phone. (1 sec.)
593. Cut back to same shot of Jefferies, talking into the phone: "That's a start; I'm at the Albert Hotel now." (2 sec.)
594. Cut back to same shot of Thorwald on the phone; the voice of Jefferies overlaps. (4 sec.)
595. Cut back to same shot of Jefferies: "I'll be looking for you." (2 sec.)
596. Cut back to same long shot of Thorwald as he puts the receiver down, puts his hat on and walks over, passing the windows, into the corridor and out. (18 sec.)
597. Cut back to two shot of the nurse and Lisa, who leaves the frame (walking from right to left). (2 sec.)
598. Cut to long shot of Jefferies in the chair. "I'll keep watch." (1 sec.)
599. Cut to long shot of the nurse and Lisa reaching the door. "One of you keep an eye on this window. If I see him coming back, I'll signal with a flashbulb." They both leave. (5 sec.)
600. Cut back to same long shot of Jefferies. He puts away the telephone book, wheels himself closer to a medium shot, picks up the

camera and starts looking. (11 sec.)
601. Cut to medium shot of the alleyway (via telephone lens). We see Thorwald as he passes through on the way to the street. (3 sec.)
602. Cut back to same medium shot of Jefferies, who wheels himself back, picks up his bag and prepares the flash equipment. (He promised to signal the women in case Thorwald comes back). He puts in a flash, wheels himself again to the window and looks down. (27 sec.)
603. Cut to high long shot of the nurse and Lisa in the garden, walking up the stairs (reminiscent of the cat walking in shot no. 3) and up a metal fire escape. Stella picks up a shovel. They start climbing. (4 sec.)
604. Cut back to same middle shot of Jefferies, looking down. (2 sec.)
605. Cut back to same long shot of Lisa and Stella, going over a fence. (2 sec.)
606. Cut back to same shot of Jefferies, looking down. (2 sec.)
607. Cut back to same shot of Lisa and the nurse, who starts digging at the rosebush in the corner. Lisa keeps watch. (10 sec.)
608. Cut back to same medium shot of Jefferies, who reaches for his phone and dials a number while watching the window. (11 sec.)
609. Cut to close medium long shot of the nurse, digging. (3 sec.)
610. Cut back to same medium shot of Jefferies, who is talking to a baby-sitter at Doyle's apartment. (19 sec.)
611. Cut back to same shot (medium long shot) of the nurse, digging. (2 sec.)
612. Cut back to same medium shot of Jefferies on the phone: "When do you expect him?" "They went to dinner and maybe night clubbin'." "I see—well, if he calls in, would you have him get in touch with L.B. Jefferies right away? I might have quite a surprise for him." He puts down the receiver. (10 sec.)
613. Cut back to long shot of the two women in the garden. Nothing has been dug up so far. (4 sec.)
614. Cut back to same shot of Jefferies, looking nervously. (2 sec.)
615. Cut to long shot of musician's studio, where a jam session is in progress. (3 sec.)

616. Cut back to same shot of Jefferies, looking. (2 sec.)
617. Cut to same shot in the garden. They're still digging. (1 sec.)
618. Cut back to same medium shot of Jefferies as he signals an encouraging gesture to Lisa. (3 sec.)
619. Cut to long shot of Lonelyhearts' window. She puts on her glasses and starts writing by the table. (7 sec.)
620. Cut back to same medium shot of Jefferies, who suddenly picks up his telephoto lens and looks down. (7 sec.)
621. Cut to the bar across the street (by telephoto lens through the alleyway), then a quick pan to the right all the way to a close-up of the nurse who gestures to Jefferies that nothing was found. (12 sec.)
622. Cut to frontal medium close-up of Jefferies as he takes the lens away, looks and worries. (5 sec.)
623. Cut to high long shot of the nurse and Lisa, who impetuously runs toward the fire-escape ladder and starts to climb up it. (6 sec.)
624. Cut back to same medium close-up of Jefferies, who anxiously cries out: "Lisa, what are you doing?" (3 sec.)
625. Cut back to same high long shot. Lisa keeps climbing; the nurse stands helplessly, then walks out of frame. (4 sec.)
626. Cut back to same shot of Jefferies, desperate. (2 sec.)
627. Cut back to same long shot of Lisa, who bravely climbs over a railing and tries to open Thorwald's small window—it won't give. (9 sec.)
628. Cut back to same medium close-up of Jefferies, crying out: "Lisa! What are you doing? Don't!" (2 sec.)
629. Cut back to same shot of Lisa, who climbs over from the balcony to Thorwald's open dining-room window, a distance of several yards. She makes it. (17 sec.)
630. Cut back to same shot of Jefferies, who, resigned, tosses his head from one side to the edge of the frame. (2 sec.)
631. Cut to long shot of Lisa, running inside Thorwald's apartment from dining room to bedroom, searching. (4 sec.)
632. Cut back to same medium close-up of Jefferies, thrusting his telephoto lens to his eye. (2 sec.)
633. Cut to closer medium shot (via telephoto) of Lisa, her back to the camera, searching in the open valise; she finds an alligator bag,

turns to the window and shows it to Jefferies (across); it turns out to be empty, and she shakes it upside down for the benefit of Jefferies. (9 sec.)
634. Cut back to same medium close-up of Jefferies as he takes away the lens, furiously shouting "Get out of there." He looks toward the alleyway to check on Thorwald. (4 sec.)
635. Cut to long shot of Lisa in the bedroom, searching in a chest of drawers. (3 sec.)
636. Cut to medium long shot of Jefferies as he suddenly turns back toward his door just as Stella comes in. She suggests he call the police. (7 sec.)
637. Cut back to same long shot of Lisa, searching the drawers. (2 sec.)
638. Cut to medium two-shot of Jefferies and Stella: "Miss Lonelyhearts. . . . " (3 sec.)
639. Cut to long shot of Lonelyhearts' shaded window. We see her looking for something, she picks up a bottle. (5 sec.)
640. Cut back to same medium two-shot. Stella: "Miss Lonelyhearts . . . Oh please, call the police." (3 sec.)
641. Cut back to same long shot of Lonelyhearts' window. She sits down. (2 sec.)
642. Cut back to same two-shot as Jefferies, on the phone, asks for the police. (1 sec.)
643. Cut back to same long shot of Lonelyhearts, who handles something that looks like pills. (7 sec.)
644. Cut back to same two-shot; Jefferies is still on the phone. (1 sec.)
645. Cut to long shot of the musician's studio, where the jam session continues. (2 sec.)
646. Cut back to same long shot of Lonelyhearts, who gets up with something in her hand. (9 sec.)
647. Cut to same long shot of Lisa (after not seeing her for the last 46 sec.). She is showing Jefferies (across) a necklace; at the same time, through the small window, Thorwald is in the corridor on his way to his door. (6 sec.)
648. Cut back to same medium two-shot. Jefferies is still on the

phone waiting to be connected to the police. *They both see Thorwald's return.* (2 sec.)
649. Cut back to same shot of Lisa. She's happy and ready to leave as Thorwald is at the door. (2 sec.)
650. Cut to low two-shot, tighter, almost in medium close-up, of Stella, her hand on her mouth and Jefferies in horror, mumbling: "Lisa, Lisa." (1 sec.)
651. Cut to tighter medium long shot of Lisa in the kitchen window; she has heard Thorwald's steps. He is just about to open the door, and she runs back to the dining room and then to the bedroom, as camera pans with her; she stops, hidden behind the wall between windows. In the windows flashes a reflection of Thorwald etntering the apartment and shutting the door. (11 sec.)
652. Cut back to same medium close-up of Stella and Jefferies; he finally has the police on the line: "A man is molesting a woman at one-two-five West Ninth Street, second floor, in the rear apartment." Policeman, off screen: "Your name or phone?" Jefferies: "L.B. Jefferies, Chelsea 2-5598." (10 sec.)
653. Cut to medium long shot of the dining-room window in Thorwald's apartment as he walks through to the bedroom; camera follows. He looks around, then notices something. (9 sec.)
654. Cut back to Jefferies' apartment, medium close-up two-shot, their two profiles frozen in horror. (1 sec.)
655. Cut back to same medium long shot of Thorwald. He picks up the bag he finds on top of the chest, thinking, then suddenly turns. (7 sec.)
656. Cut to close-up of Jefferies, frozen in fear. (1 sec.)
657. Cut back to same long shot of Thorwald's windows. He saw Lisa, starts walking toward her and disappears behind the wall (separating the windows). Lisa emerges in the dining-room window as she backs out from him. She holds something behind her back, and is talking and gesticulating. Thorwald follows her. They face each other in profile. (13 sec.)
658. Cut back to same close-up of Jefferies, the nurse's forearm on his shoulder. He swallows. (2 sec.)
659. Cut to medium long shot of Thorwald's dining-room window

as Thorwald grabs Lisa and pulls her down. (2 sec.)
660. Cut back to same close-up of Jefferies, reacting with a cry. (4 sec.)
661. Cut back to same shot of Thorwald's window. Lisa is down, almost out of frame. Thorwald shouts and demands she give him the object she is hiding. (6 sec.)
662. Cut back to same shot of Jefferies, who breathes heavily. Stella seems to be clamping onto him. (4 sec.)
663. Cut back to same shot of Thorwald's window. Lisa gets up; Thorwald seizes her and starts shaking her. (5 sec.)
664. Cut back to same close-up of Jefferies, who reacts violently: "No, no, oh!" (3 sec.)
665. Cut back to same shot of Thorwald's window. He keeps shaking her. She defends herself, and screams. (2 sec.)
666. On the scream, cut to same close-up of Jefferies, who, tears in his eyes, leans back and covers his mouth. (3 sec.)
667. Cut back to same medium long shot of Thorwald's window. The struggle continues. Thorwald turns off the light. (3 sec.)
668. Cut back to same close-up of Jefferies, who turns his face away and then back again: "Stella, what are we going to do?" (4 sec.)
669. Cut back to same shot of Thorwald's window. The struggle continues in the dark, with bright highlights. (2 sec.)
670. Cut back to same shot of Jefferies, who grabs his neck with both hands. Off screen, Stella says: "Look, police coming." (2 sec.)
671. Cut to wider long shot of all of Thorwald's windows. The light in the corridor is on. A policeman with others behind is approaching. In the dark window the struggle continues. (3 sec.)
672. Cut to medium two-shot of Stella and Jefferies, who are relieved. (2 sec.)
673. Cut back to same long shot of the windows. The policemen ring the bell. Thorwald puts the light on. Lisa is getting up from the kneeling position. Thorwald starts moving toward the door. (10 sec.)
674. Cut to higher medium shot of the nurse and Jefferies who look on. (2 sec.)
675. Cut back to same long shot of Thorwald's windows. Thorwald is just about to open the door, and looks back to Lisa. She straightens

herself out. (3 sec.)
676. Cut back to same two-shot, as Jefferies takes his camera, with telephoto lens, to his eye. (2 sec.)
677. Cut to close medium shot (via telephoto) of Thorwald, who, in his blue jacket, opens the door, pale, amazed to face the police (who are not yet seen since they are out of frame). He turns again to Lisa and he points in her direction, presumably accusing her of intrusion and theft. So far Thorwald is the only one in the frame. (10 sec.)
678. Cut back to same high two-shot; Jefferies still holds the lens, then puts it away. (2 sec.)
679. Cut to wide long shot of Thorwald's windows. The police enter with Thorwald behind. Lisa is in the middle of the dining room. The police approach Lisa, who is now with her back to the camera. Thorwald shows the purse to another policeman. (9 sec.)
680. Cut back to same high two-shot. Stella walks behind the wheelchair. They both look. Jefferies lifts up his lens. (8 sec.)
681. Cut to medium shot (via telephoto) of the dining-room window. The group surrounds Lisa. Thorwald, on the right, keeps showing the purse. (2 sec.)
682. Cut back to same two-shot. Jefferies looks through his telephoto, while the nurse watches with binoculars. (2 sec.)
683. Cut back to same medium shot of the window. Thorwald explains something to the policeman on the right, Lisa talks to the one on the left. (6 sec.)
684. Cut to single medium close-up of Jefferies, looking through the lens. (1.5 sec.)
685. Cut to a close-up of Lisa (via telephoto), her back to the camera. She points, for the benefit of Jefferies, to a wedding ring on her finger. Camera pans down to the ring then pans fast to the face of Thorwald, who notices her gestures; he looks across toward Jefferies' window. He has figured it out. (9 sec.)
686. Cut to medium shot of Jefferies, who suddenly pulls his chair back and turns to Stella: "Turn off the lights . . . He sees?" The nurse walks over, the room darkens. (5 sec.)
687. Cut back to long shot of Thorwald's windows. The police start moving out of Thorwald's apartment. They take Lisa. (4 sec.)

688. Cut to medium shot of Jefferies, who pulls his chair back: "How long will they be there?" He asks the nurse to hand him his wallet—he needs money for bailing Lisa out of jail—and counts the money. "Yeah—let's see—a hundred and twenty-seven dollars." Nurse: "How much do you need?" Jefferies: "Well—first offense burglary—that's about two hundred and fifty." Nurse: "Lisa's handbag!" Jefferies: "How much does she have?" Stella: "Hmpfh! Fifty cents!" Jefferies: "Here, take this." Nurse: "Look, I got twenty dollars or so in my purse." Jefferies: "Give me what you've got." (35 sec.)
689. Cut to closer medium close-up of Jefferies as he gives her the money: "Take this." (3 sec.)
690. Cut back to long shot of Thorwald's windows in the dark. Corridor light is on. Thorwald starts moving to go out and looks across. (3 sec.)
691. Cut to medium shot of Jefferies, who rolls his chair to the phone, and starts dialing. (7 sec.)
692. Cut to a medium long shot of the nurse. She goes out. (2 sec.)
693. Cut to medium close-up of Jefferies, on the phone; camera moves closer as he speaks frantically to Doyle's voice: "All right—what is it now?" Jefferies: "Doyle, I've got something really big for you!" Doyle: "Why did I have to return your call? Look, Jeff, don't louse up my night with another mad killer stuffing a grisly trunk. . . . " Jefferies: "Listen to me! Listen to me! Lisa's in jail! She got arrested!" Doyle's voice: "Your Lisa?" Jefferies: "My Lisa. Boy you should have seen her! She got into Thorwald's apartment—but then he came back and the only way I could get her out was to call the police." Doyle's voice: "I told you . . . . " "I know you told me! She went in to get evidence and she came out with evidence." Doyle's voice: "Like what?" Jefferies: "Like Mrs. Thorwald's wedding ring. That's like what. If that woman was alive, she'd be wearing that ring. Right?" Doyle: "A possibility." Jefferies: "A possibility? It's a fact! He killed a dog last night because the dog was scratching around in the garden. You know why? Because he had something buried in that garden that the dog scented." Doyle's voice: "Like an old ham bone?" Jefferies: "Look, I don't know what pet names Thorwald had for his wife, but I'll tell you this: All those trips at night with that

metal suitcase—he wasn't taking out his possessions, because his possessions are still up in the apartment." Doyle's voice: "Perhaps it was an old ham bone!" Jefferies: "Yeah, in sections. And I'll tell you something else. All the telephone calls he made were long distance. All right, now, if he called his wife long distance on the day she left—after she arrived in Merritsville—why did she write a card to him, sayin' that she'd arrived in Merritsville? Why did she do that?" Doyle's voice: "Where'd they take Lisa?" Jefferies: "Precinct Six. I sent somebody over with bail money." The conversation is in hushed tones. Finally, Doyle promises to run over. Jefferies hangs up, looks into the window across; he approaches camera, in close-up. (long duration). (1 min., 37 sec.)
694. Cut back to same long shot of Thorwald's windows. It's still dark, without any life. (3 sec.)
695. Cut to medium close-up of Jefferies. His phone is ringing, he picks it up and starts talking: "I think Thorwald has left," then realizes that it is not the detective. He moves the receiver a couple of inches away, scared, listening to a void. The other party clicks down, disconnects. Jefferies, in terror, looks across and around—a faint sound of steps can be heard. Camera moves in, into a close-up. (44 sec.)
696. Cut to medium shot of Jefferies' door, dark except for the bottom, where the corridor light penetrates. (1 sec.)
697. Cut to high close-up of Jefferies from the back; he turns his chair to face the door, penetratingly looking and thinking. (20 sec.)
698. Cut back to same shot of the door. Light at the bottom. (2 sec.)
699. Cut to medium long shot of Jefferies in profile as he suddenly turns his wheelchair to the right, then to the left, backing out, then, after hesitation, moving forward. Finally, he is with his back to the camera. (18 sec.)
700. Cut to reverse medium shot of Jefferies, facing camera, close to the steps leading to his door. (7 sec.)
701. Cut on action to medium close-up. He tries to get out of his wheelchair. Steps are heard outside. Jefferies sinks back into his wheelchair—he is trapped. (8 sec.)
702. Cut to closer shot of the bottom part of Jefferies' door; the light goes out. (3 sec.)

703. Cut back to same medium close-up of Jefferies, in horror and fear; he looks around, then backs his chair away to a medium long shot. He searches and finally pulls out from the side of his chair the flash equipment. (21 sec.)
704. Cut on action to close-up of the equipment and the box of bulbs being prepared for use. (3 sec.)
705. Cut on action to medium long shot of Jefferies, as he starts backing his wheelchair all the way to his window (becoming a long shot by now). The steps are loud and near. (11 sec.)
706. Cut to the dark door (in medium long shot). (2 sec.)
707. Cut back to same medium shot of Jefferies, who is in suspense. (3 sec.)
708. Cut to long shot of the door. At first dark, then, as it slowly opens, the figure of Thorwald moves in, heavily backlit, sweaty, with glasses, ominous. (14 sec.)
709. Cut to high long shot of Jefferies. His window backlights him. (3 sec.)
710. Cut to Thorwald in long shot, in the dark, except for a small highlight on top of his head. He addresses Jefferies, slowly, in a chilling, deep voice: "What do you want from me?" (4 sec.)
711. Cut back to same high long shot of Jefferies, in his chair. (2 sec.)
712. Cut back to same long shot of Thorwald: "...And the girl... She could have turned me in... Why didn't she?" (6 sec.)
713. Cut back to same shot of Jefferies, motionless. (3 sec.)
714. Cut back to same long shot of Thorwald: "What is it that you want?... A lot of money,... I don't have any money." (7 sec.)
715. Cut back to same long shot of Jefferies, waiting. (2 sec.)
716. Cut back to same long shot of Thorwald: "Say something." (4 sec.)
717. Cut back to same shot of Jefferies, still. (1 sec.)
718. Cut back to same shot of Thorwald: "Can you get me that ring back?" (5 sec.)
719. Cut back to same shot of Jefferies: "No." He is starting to insert a bulb into the flash. Thorwald says: "Tell her to bring it back." Jefferies: "The police have it by now." (8 sec.)

720. Cut back to same shot of Thorwald, who starts moving forward. (2 sec.)
721. Cut to dramatically low medium shot of Jefferies (diagonal in the frame, face in three-quarter profile, his cast is in the left foreground). He lifts his hand and fires a bulb with blinding flash, at the same time covering his own face. (2 sec.)
722. Cut to Thorwald (same long shot), who moves in blue light for a half-second, then dark. (2 sec.)
723. Cut on action to close-up of Thorwald in the dark, then in a pink-red explosion, an aftereffect of the flash, that envelops the frame. (3 sec.)
724. Cut to the same long shot of Jefferies—the remnant of the pink-red is over him too—as he prepares the next bulb for a flash. (3 sec.)
725. Cut to medium close-up of Thorwald, who, still rubbing his eyes, takes another step down. (1 sec.)
726. Cut back to same long shot of Jefferies, who looks back toward his window, then inserts the new bulb. New explosion. Blue light. (3.5 sec.)
727. Cut to long shot of Thorwald in blue light (a few frames). (0.5 sec.)
728. Cut to same medium close-up of Thorwald, rubbing his eyes, adjusting his glasses and moving forward. A new explosion of pink-red, as before, blinds him. (2 sec.)
729. Cut to medium long shot of Jefferies; the pink-red fades away, he is preparing the next bulb; again he looks back, covers his face. (2 sec.)
730. Cut to same medium close-up of Thorwald, taking another step. (1 sec.)
731. Cut to medium shot of Jefferies (he is getting closer to camera) preparing another bulb; he leans back as if to escape. (1 sec.)
732. Cut to full long shot of Thorwald as he takes another step, then a new explosion; he puts his hands up, but moves forward. (2 sec.)
733. Cut to close-up of Thorwald, adjusting his glasses as the pink-red takes over. (1 sec.)
734. Cut to same medium shot of Jefferies, readying the next bulb. (1 sec.)

735. Cut to medium close-up of Thorwald, taking yet another step. (1 sec.)
736. Cut to same medium shot of Jefferies, covering his eyes. (1 sec.)
737. Cut to medium shot of Thorwald in the blue flash; he takes another step forward—red-pink takes over. (1 sec.)
738. Cut on action to close-up of Thorwald, who is in the after-shock of the blinding flash; he wipes his glasses. (1 sec.)
739. Cut to same medium shot of Jefferies—red-pink fades. (1 sec.)
740. Cut to new close-up of Jefferies, looking desperately back. (1 sec.)
741. Cut to long shot of the small window in Thorwald's apartment, showing the corridor where people and police crowd in. Jefferies, off screen, cries: "Lisa, Lisa!" (2 sec.)
742. Cut to medium close-up of Thorwald, bolting forward. Jefferies: "Doyle!" (1 sec.)
743. Cut on action to medium two-shot. Thorwald starts choking Jefferies. (The highlights come from the window.) (2 sec.)
744. Cut back to same long shot of the corridor window with the crowd of people and police moving to the door. (2 sec.)
745. Cut to medium close-up of Thorwald on top of Jefferies, struggling. (2 sec.)
746. Cut to close-up of Jefferies, being choked. (1 sec.)
747. Quick cut to long shot of the window across. (0.5 sec.)
748. Cut to close-up of the struggle. Thorwald on the left, Jefferies on the right. (1 sec.)
749. Cut to medium shot of the struggle; Jefferies being lifted. (2 sec.)
750. Cut to close-up of Jefferies' head falling. (0.5 sec.)
751. Cut to close-up of Thorwald, moving forward. (0.5 sec.)
752-758. Six cuts, a half second or less, of different parts of the body; Jefferies' cast, Thorwald's arms, etc. (3 sec. total)
759. Cut to long shot of a couple on the fire escape, looking. (0.5 sec.)
760. Cut to medium shot of Thorwald, throwing Jefferies over the windowsill. (2 sec.)
761-768. Seven cuts of a half second or less of Jefferies' body, face,

shirt in desperate movements. (3.5 sec.)
769. Cut to long shot of Lonelyhearts, stepping out on the fire escape. (0.5 sec.)
770-774. Five shots in close-up or extreme close-up of the final struggle: Thorwald's face, Jefferies' face in extreme close-up, hands holding the sill, Thorwald again in close-up, Jefferies' eyes desperately bulging, Thorwald's hands pushing, Jefferies' hand on the sill (in extreme close-up). (2.5 sec.)
775. Cut to medium long shot of the newlyweds, looking out their little window. (1.5 sec.)
776. Cut to medium long shot of a group of police and others, including the detective, entering the garden level, running across, as camera follows, climbing the short fence; the camera pans to Jefferies' window; in long shot, his body hangs down as Thorwald tries to push him down. *[Note: This is the first time Jefferies' window is seen from the outside.]* (9 sec.)
777. Cut to high exterior medium shot of a group of police, running. They cry: "Give me your .38." A gun is thrown and caught. (5 sec.)
778. Cut to reverse close long shot of Jefferies hanging on. In the foreground someone is pointing a gun at Thorwald. (1 sec.)
779. Cut to close exterior medium shot of Jefferies' window. A plainclothesman is pulling Thorwald away, as Jefferies still hangs on. (1 sec.)
780. Cut to reverse (interior) high medium shot of Jefferies. He lets go and falls out of the frame. (1.5 sec.)
781. Cut to reverse exterior medium long shot (from inside looking out) as Jefferies falls into the arms of waiting police. (0.5 sec.)
782-784. Three brief shots—each less than a half second. Close-up of Jefferies' hand landing on the cement, medium shot of part of his body, from a 90° angle, arms of the policeman. (1.5 sec.)
785. Cut to medium long shot of a group, including the detective Doyle, running toward Jefferies; camera follows. They reach him in medium shot. He lifts his head. The nurse and Lisa come into the frame. (8 sec.)
786. Cut on action to medium close-up of Lisa, lifting Jefferies' face.

Jefferies: "Oh, Lisa, sweet, if anything had happened to you!" Lisa: "Oh, you shut up—I'm all right." (3 sec.)
787. Cut to close-up of Jefferies' laughing face, Lisa's hands on his cheeks. He talks to her: "I'm proud of you." He then turns (to where the detective is standing out of frame): "Now you'll file for a search warrant?" (9 sec.)
788. Cut to low medium shot of the detective Doyle, answering: "Oh, yes . . . . " He is being called from behind, gets up and looks, then says: "He is alive." (6 sec.)
789. Cut to exterior medium shot of Jefferies' window. Another plainclothesman is saying to Doyle below: "Thorwald's ready to take us on a tour of the East River." (7 sec.)
790. Cut to low medium shot of the detective and Stella, looking up as the voice from above continues about Thorwald's confession. (5 sec.)
791. Cut to close-up of the two as the nurse says something into the detective's ear. He in turn looks up and asks: "Was the body buried in this flower bed?" (7 sec.)
792. Cut to low medium shot of the plainclothesman up in the window: "Yeah, the dog got too inquisitive, so he dug it up. It's in a hat box up in the apartment. (8 sec.)
793. Cut to close-up of the nurse, amazed. (2 sec.)
794. Cut to close-up of detective Doyle, asking the nurse: "Do you want to have a look?" (2 sec.)
795. Cut back to same close-up of the nurse, who hesitantly says: "No, I don't want to have any part in it!" (6 sec.)
FADE-OUT.
796. *FADE-IN.* Sometime later. Close-up of the thermometer, showing 70°F; after a brief hold, the camera starts panning to the left, first to the musician's studio; the musician is talking to Miss Lonelyhearts, who is mouthing that she loves his song, upon which the musician puts a record into a player and they both sit down to listen. Music, a voice sings: "Lisa, with your daffodil April face Lisa, full of starry-eyed laughing grace; Hold me and whisper the sweet words I'm yearning for; Drown me in kisses, Caresses I'm burning for." Lonelyhearts seems to be happy. The music is the familiar song heard

before, and continues to the end of the shot. Camera starts panning again to the left, and soon reaches the windows of Thorwald's former apartment; house painters with rollers are repainting the room. Camera keeps panning to the fire-escape balcony; the dog owner is putting a new dog in the basket; camera pans over to the dancer's window, where she is dancing as usual. Then she stops; the door opens for a short, bespectacled GI. She exclaims: "Stanley!" and runs to him, kisses and hugs him passionately; she helps him to unload, they talk. Her boyfriend or husband has come home. Camera continues panning down to the sculptress' doorway, and, farther left, she is sleeping in her chaise longue. Camera pans to the left wall where the lady puts out the cage with the birds (in symmetry to the beginning of the film). Camera pans up and left past the newlyweds' window, where inside he is sitting at the table as she serves him coffee. Camera swings left, finally reaching Jefferies' window. He is sleeping in his wheelchair, blissfully, with a smile on his face. Camera pans down to his cast: Both legs have a cast now, two pairs of toes sticking out, comically. Camera keeps panning to the right to a pair of woman's legs, up to Lisa, who is reclining on the couch by the window, reading a book about the Himalayas.

She checks to see if Jefferies is sleeping. Then, she sneakily picks up *Harper's Bazaar* magazine and reads it with savor. *FADE-OUT.*

FADE-IN. Long shot, as in shot no. 1. Bamboo curtain rolls down.

"END" credit superimposed. "A Paramount Release" *FADE-OUT.* (1 min., 42 sec.)

Total time: 1 hour, 48 minutes.

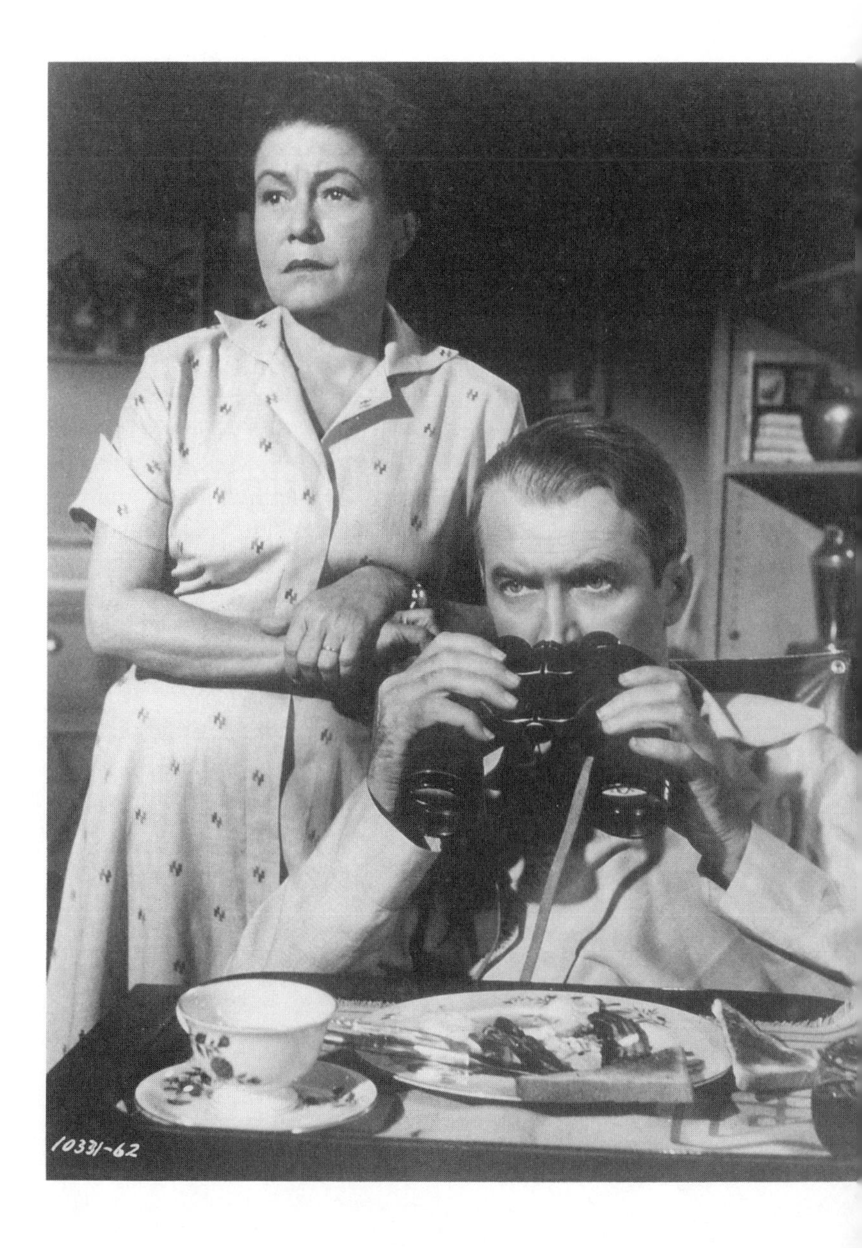
10331-62

5

CONCLUDING REMARKS

In readdressing the question of voyeurism, it is clear that the protagonist in *Rear Window* may be a Peeping Tom, but he is not a pervert. Hitchcock justifies Jefferies' voyeurism by his condition; he is confined to a wheelchair with nothing else to do. What's more, a summer heat wave rages on, and everyone's window is open. Jefferies' "peeping" is of the normal kind to which cinema as a visual medium is especially susceptible. The voyeuristic drive is an unavoidable part of watching a film. Moreover, Hitchcock is creating a critique of voyeurism. As he told François Truffaut: "I'll bet you nine out of ten people, if they see a woman across the courtyard undressing for bed ... will stay and look; no one turns away and says: it's none of my business. They could pull down their blinds, but they never do; they stand looking out."[1]

According to Sigmund Freud, "Voyeurism has its origins in one of the component instincts, the scopophilic instinct...voyeurism functions not only in perversion but also in more normal behavior of seeing and being seen, in various ways of everyday life."[2]

Jefferies does indeed indulge in the pleasure of looking; at times he questions his own behavior, but never that strongly, even ignoring remonstrations from his girlfriend Lisa. At the end Hitchcock redeems his Peeping Tom by making him the hero of a crime drama, at the risk of his life.

Turning to this study's major subject, cinema art in general, this integrated single work has given me the opportunity to elaborate on the consistency of certain forms and harmonies. The intention here has not been to canonize Hitchcock or this film in particular, but rather to turn attention to certain theoretical aspects contained therein, especially the large number of silent passages. Hitchcock probably would agree with the proposition that contemporary cinema as an art form takes its origins not from when sound on film was invented

---

[1] *Hitchcock,* by François Truffaut (Simon and Schuster, 1967); pages 159-169.

[2] Sigmund Freud, *Complete Works.*

but instead from the silent-film era, including its morphogenic stages.[3]

Perhaps it was in order to restore the legitimacy or breathe new life into the silent screen that Hitchcock embarked on a project offering him, as he told Truffaut, "a possibility of doing a purely cinematic film: you have an immobilized man looking out. That's one part of the film. The second part shows what he sees and the third part shows how he reacts. This is actually the purest expression of a cinema idea."[4]

As mentioned earlier, 35 percent of *Rear Window* is totally silent, and an additional 15 percent can be considered semi-silent, as when Jefferies and his companions watch across while commenting on what they see. The statistical facts are themselves surprising. Hitchcock handled those silent sections masterfully, balancing adeptly between the second-hand voyeurism, i.e., subjective viewing under the guidance of Jefferies, and the objective one, when Jefferies does not look. Consequently, he creates a complex dichotomy between two modes of perception, which eventually converge at the end of the film.

Another important modality in this film is the directorial strategy: the immaculate planning and orchestration of its various elements of structure. It is reminiscent, as I have stated elsewhere[5], of an architect's plans. There, all stresses have to be figured out ahead of time, then harmonized with scores of correlates, never losing control of the overall aesthetic thrust. Hitchcock's strategies also recall music composition with their rhythms and harmonies. As can be seen in the

---

[3] Of the silent era, Thomas Mann, in *The Magic Mountain,* wrote: "Life flitted across the screen before their smarting eyes: life chopped into small sections, fleeting, accelerated; a restless, jerky fluctuation of appearing and disappearing, performed to a thin accompaniment of music, which set its actual *tempo* to the phantasmagoria of the past, and with the narrowest of means at its command, yet managed to evoke a whole gamut of pomp and solemnity, passion, abandon, and gurgling sensuality. It was a thrilling drama of love and death they saw silently reeled off."

[4] *Hitchcock,* Truffaut.

[5] Sharff, 91.

body of this analysis, Hitchcock populated this film with an array of symmetries and subsymmetries, contrapuntal arrangements, trigger-releases, slow disclosures, familiar images and those ominous transitions by way of fades; each scene is woven out from these elements, and their presence is detectable in different combinations—they are the poetics of his cinema.

Most important, Hitchcock knew how to frame a shot, i.e., where to place the camera. Yet in each instance the structure of the element determined the mode of framing, not necessarily according to the needs of the plot. For example, when a cinematic symmetry was created for Lisa's coming to and leaving Jefferies' apartment, both her arrival and departure are symmetrically in long shots (Lisa taking off her gloves at the beginning and putting them on again at the end). In one scene, after a heated argument, Lisa tells Jefferies before leaving: "I'm in love with you." This occasion usually would call for a close-up, to enhance her pronouncement. But here it was bypassed, for it would ruin the symmetry. Furthermore, this example, and many similar ones in the film, prove that spoon-feeding close-ups in order to sweeten confessions of love or of emotional states, as practiced profusely in many contemporary films, is not necessary and is counterproductive: these close-ups overpopulate the screen with "big faces" and, consequently, desensitize the audience to them.

Hitchcock avoids overusing close shots, distributing them carefully in his chain of shots to fit his harmonies. He never considered the close-up as a vehicle for actorial virtuosity. Indeed, he is not known for being an actor's director; by his own admission, he was tough with actors. He jokingly told my students that he requires actors to do exactly what they are told and that their motivation for the performance should be their pay. Interestingly enough, in *Rear Window* there are hardly any long-duration shots to allow an actor a sustained performance. Hitchcock's propensity to fragment is by itself antagonistic to actorial soliloquizing. The closest examples to such a soliliquy are the two scenes when Jefferies uses his back-scratcher to try to calm down an annoying itch inside his cast; Jimmy Stewart does it hilariously, with the help of Hitchcock's ingenious framing: a medium long shot, his naked toe wiggling in the fore-

ground, facing the camera. In general, one can safely state that all the performances in this film are exemplary. However, it is important to emphasize that Hitchcock's precise framing and his singular placement of shots, especially in the fragmented sections, are not only complementary by designing actorial performances but they also become the scene's quintessential driving force. No wonder Jimmy Stewart stated some time ago, in an interview with The New York Times, that upon seeing *Rear Window* he did not remember playing the way he saw it on the screen. The structured cinema language is unbound here from the theatrical expressions.

The film is, likewise, independent from its literary progenitor; *Rear Window* is freewheelingly adapted (screenplay by M. Haynes) from a minor short story by Cornell Woodrich of the same title. Only a skeletal core of the short story was used: the looking and the crime discovery. The original short story did not contain any love relationship or community involvement. *Rear Window* has a complex narrative structure with many parallel actions between the main plot and the silent subplots, sandwiched in between and around, chasing each other fuguelike in various tempos and intensities—in sum, a construct with ample cinema sense.[6]

The most striking illustration of that cinema sense is the singular impact of the "fourth-wall shot" of Jefferies hanging down from his window (shot no. 776). This reverse long shot is of great importance, for it tells legions, cinematically, about film viewing as well as visual perception; it presents a rare occasion of seeing the holy grail of an illusion fulfilled, with a flair. The situation is simple: through a montage of brief shots, mostly close ones, we witness how our protagonist is attacked, beaten and almost thrown out of his window, still clinging for dear life to the sill (ironically enough, the same win-

---

[6] Hitchcock to Truffaut: "I don't care about the subject matter; I don't care about the acting; but I do care about the pieces of film and the photography and the soundtrack and all of the technical ingredients. . . ." Quoted in *The New York Times*, February 1985.

dow from which he has been looking out). All of the above shots are taken from the inside of his room. Then, suddenly, like a revelation, our eyes are struck by this reverse long shot of Jefferies hanging down seen from the outside! The audience reacts to it viscerally. Its strength is derived mainly from the delay of its appearance, held over to almost the end of the film. In fact, this spectacular long shot (no. 776) does not deliver any new narrative information, since we already know of Jefferies' predicament. Yet, as with all the imagery of Jefferies looking across, we only assume and believe that there is "a there" there: a real wall on the other side of his window. That unquestioning assumption was subliminally suspended like an illusion waiting for some sort of resolution. The fourth wall long shot shows for the first time that there indeed is an outside wall, and thus clarifies the assumption once and for all. Finally, the community of the courtyard sees Jefferies, and we, the audience, see them seeing him. Jefferies' domination of the looking is broken and, thanks to the inversion of view, we see him objectively. One should also keep in mind that the fourth wall resolution renders a nonproscenium way of looking, a faculty exclusive to cinema, as opposed to the proscenium-type viewing in the theater, where the audience itself *is* the fourth wall. In *Rear Window*, this slow disclosure, for it is within that element of structure, is given a classical dimension and a purely cinesthetic solution; it seems like a visual discovery, almost a new sensation.

No doubt there are other ways of looking at cinema—the phenomenon of the screen is complex beyond what one would expect from a popular art. Yet, considering the sheer gravity of influence it exerts on our culture, it is gratifying to discover that the "bricks and mortar" of its construct contains the resources for a higher reach, not unlike in the other arts.

I hope I have persuaded the reader of the close and genuine relationship between harmonious structures and the aesthetics of a high-vernacular visual language. Here, we have seen how in a mainstream film like *Rear Window,* embellished with marquee-value performers, a master filmmaker focused mainly on "pure cinema expression."

GLOSSARY

TERMS IN italicized capitals are cross references defined alphabetically. All terms are explained in reference to their screen effect unless otherwise specified.

ACCELERATED MOTION: A stuffy term for Fast Motion.

AFTER-IMAGE: An image so graphically strong that the mind's eye retains it even though a new shot has appeared on the screen.

ASPECT RATIO: The shape of the overall picture—so-called because screen shape is identified by the ratio of the screen's width to its height. Screen shapes vary from the normal, nearly square, ratio of 1.33:1 to very long rectangles. (The ratio of most of today's wide screens is 1.85:1) In the 1950s Hollywood began to compete with various kinds of wide-screen systems, such as Cinemascope, Cinerama, and Vistavision. If a director is preparing a scene which will not look good in a wide-screen format, he may use natural blocking to reframe the image. For example, he may shoot through curtains or doorways that are ostensibly part of the set but appear dark in the foreground.

AVAILABLE LIGHTING: see *LIGHTING.*

CINEMA VÉRITÉ: An approach to film-making that tries not to interfere with reality. It plays down the technical and formal means of production (script, special lighting, etc.) at the director's disposal and emphasizes the circumstantial reality of the scenes. It often uses natural sound, *AVAILABLE LIGHTING,* and conspicuous camera work (e.g. *ZOOM* and *HAND-HELD SHOTS*), since flexibility is considered more essential than perfection of technique. The term is applied to the documentary work of Jean Rouch, the Maysles, Richard Leacock and others.

CIRCULAR CAMERA MOVEMENT: See *SHOT.*

CLOSE-UP: See *SHOT.*

CONTINUITY CUTTING: A style of editing marked by its emphasis on maintaining the continuous and seemingly uninterrupted

flow of action in a story. However, the continuous time is apparent, not *REAL TIME* (as within the long takes of *CINEMA VÉRITÉ*, for example). Contrasted with *DYNAMIC CUTTING*.
CROSS-CUTTING: Switching back and forth between two or more scenes—for example, a serial episode that alternately shows the heroine nearing the waterfall and the hero galloping to the rescue. Cross-cutting can create *PARALLEL ACTION*, time, and space. In cases like the above last-minute rescue, excitement and tension are often increased by shortening the shots and accelerating the rhythm of the cross-cutting.
CROSSING THE AXIS: If we draw a line (axis) through the main action of a scene, any camera position on one side of the line will preserve screen direction. If a car is traveling left to right and the camera were to *CROSS THE AXIS* and shoot from side B, the car would appear to travel right to left. Crossing the axis is a beginner's "no-no" because the results can be ambiguous. However, any number of great directors have proven that they can preserve our sense of a single direction despite the opposite movements.
CUT: A *TRANSITION* made by splicing two pieces of film together. Types of cutting defined in this glossary include: *CONTINUITY CUTTING, CROSS-CUTTING, CUTAWAY, CUTTING ON ACTION, DYNAMIC CUTTING, FORM CUT, HIDDEN CUT, JUMP-CUT, SEPARATION.*
CUTAWAY: A shot of short duration that supposedly takes place at the same time as the main action, but not directly involved in the main action. For examples of cutaways, see *REACTION SHOT* and *INSERT SHOT*. Cutaways are sometimes used less for artistic purposes than to overcome continuity gaps when some footage is bad or missing. If the president picked his teeth while speaking, a sympathetic editor would keep the sound but visually cut away to a shot of someone listening that was taken earlier to cover up such routine mishaps.
CUTTING ON ACTION: Cutting from one shot to another view that "matches" it in action and gives the impression of a continuous time span. Example: the actor begins to sit down in a *MEDIUM SHOT* and finishes in a *CLOSE-UP*. By having an actor begin a

gesture in one shot and carry it through to completion in the next, the director creates a visual bridge which distracts us from noticing the cut.

DECELERATED MOTION: A stuffy term for *SLOW MOTION.*

DEEP FOCUS: See *FOCUS.*

DISSOLVE: See *TRANSITIONS.*

DOLLY SHOT: see *SHOT*

DYNAMIC CUTTING: A type of editing which, by the juxtaposition of contrasting shots or sequences, generates ideas in the viewer's mind which were not latent in the shots themselves. Simplified example: shot of man + shot of peacock = idea of egomaniac. Eisenstein thought of *MONTAGE* as this kind of creative editing.

ESTABLISHING SHOT: See *SHOT.*

EXPRESSIONISM: A mode of shooting developed in Germany during the 1920s (e.g. The Cabinet of Dr. Caligari) which used highly unnaturalistic lighting, sets, makeup, acting, etc., to give a dramatic, larger-than-life effect. Its influence on American films can be seen in Ford's *The Informer* and Welles' *Citizen Kane.*

EXTREME CLOSE-UP: See *SHOT.*

EYE-LEVEL SHOT: See *SHOT*

FADE: See *TRANSITIONS.*

FAMILIAR IMAGE: A graphically strong shot that repeats itself with little change during a film. The repetition has a subliminal effect, creating a visual abstract thought. A familar image both serves as a stabilizing bridge to the action and accrues meaning as the film progresses. Examples include the "cradle endlessly rocking" in *Intolerance* and the *LOW-ANGLE SHOT* of Patton against the sky, in *Patton.*

FAST MOTION: Action that appears faster on the screen than it could in reality. Frequently used in the silent film chase. This special effect is shot by running the camera more slowly than usual (e.g., at 12 frames per second instead of the normal 24 for sound films). Since camera and projection speeds were not standardized until the silent era was almost over, we now often see silent films at a much faster speed than we were meant to. Thus we find an unintentional comic effect.

FLAT LIGHTING: See *LIGHTING.*

FOCUS: An object in focus has a sharp and well-defined image. If it is out of focus it appears blurred. Focus is mainly affected by the lens of the camera, the projector, and your eye.

- *DEEP FOCUS:* In deep focus, objects in the immediate foreground and at great distance appear in equally sharp focus at the same time.
- *SELECTIVE FOCUS:* In selective focus, the main object of interest is in focus, the remainder of the objects are out of focus. It is (too) often used when the two lovers gamboling in focus through the fields are photographed through a foreground of out-of-focus flowers.
- *SOFT-FOCUS:* In soft focus, often used for romantic effects, all objects appear blurred because none are perfectly in focus. This diffused effect is often used to photograph aging leading ladies. Soft focus can be obtained with filters as well as lenses.
- *FOLLOW FOCUS:* If the camera or the subject moves during the shot, the camera may have to be refocused during the take in order to keep the subject in focus. The procedure is called follow-focus.
- *SEARCH FOCUS:* Also called "rack focus." The switching of focus within a shot from one person or thing to another. For instance, in filming a conversation between two people, the director can place them in the same frame, one in the foreground and one in the background, and alternately keep one in focus, the other out of focus. This is a popular TV effect.

FORM CUT: Framing in a successive shot an object which has a shape or contour similar to an image in the immediately preceding shot. In Griffith's *Intolerance,* for example, the camera cuts from Belshazzar's round shield to the round end of a battering ram pounding the city gates. The circumference and location in the frame of the two circles are identical.

FRAME: See *UNITS OF FILM LENGTH.*

FREEZE FRAME: The effect in which action appears to come to a dead stop. This is accomplished by printing one frame many times. TV's instant replay sometimes "freezes" a crucial action to let us get a better look at it (But this is done electronically, not with film).

Freezes are a popular way to end today's movies, to give an existential feeling rather than a sense of finality. Among the better examples are the zoom-freezes that end *The 400 Blows* and *Wanda.*

GRAPHICS: The formal structured content of the cine-image, as opposed to the haphazard arrangement of the narrative contents.

HAND-HELD SHOT: A shot made with the camera not mounted on a tripod or other stabilizing fixture. Since it gains flexibility while it loses stability, it is often used for *CINEMA VÉRITÉ.*

HIDDEN CUT: An inconspicuous cut, usually used in a fast-action scene, with which the director accelerates the action without significantly shifting the angle or distance as required for a more noticeable cut.

HIGH-ANGLE SHOT: see *SHOT.*

INSERT SHOT: A CUTAWAY shot inserted for the purpose of giving the audience a closer look at what the character on the screen is seeing or doing; e.g., we see a *MEDIUM SHOT* of the actor raising his wrist and looking at his watch; then an *EXTREME CLOSE-UP* shot of the watch face; then a medium shot of the actor finishing looking at the watch and lowering his wrist.

IRIS: See *TRANSITIONS.*

JUMP-CUT: A cut that jumps forward from one part of an action to another separated from the first by an interval of time. It thus creates geographical dislocation with a unity of space. It usually connects the beginning and ending of an action, leaving out the middle. Godard's *Breathless* created a 60s vogue for jump-cuts.

LIGHTING: The distribution of light and how it models the subjects and affects the graphics is the main aesthetic element of film other than composition.

Light can be natural (sunlit) or artificial (electric). It can be flat (not highly contrasted in brights and darks) or highlight. Highlights create dramatic graphic effects. Low-key lighting is recognized by the absence of a strong source of light from a defined direction which creates highlights.

When extra lights are not brought along for shooting, as is often the case with *CINEMA VÉRITÉ, AVAILABLE LIGHTING* (whatever is normally there) is used.

Most film stocks are not "fast" enough to shoot an ordinary outdoor night scene. So the scene is shot in the daylight and filters are added to darken the scene to look like night. This is called shooting *day for night*. Similarly, there are aesthetic reasons for shooting *night for day, exterior for interior,* and *interior for exterior.*

LOCATION: Any place, other than the studio or studio lot, where a film is shot.

LONG SHOT: See *SHOT.*

LOW-ANGLE SHOT: See *SHOT.*

LOW-KEY LIGHTING: See *LIGHTING.*

MASTER SHOT: See *SHOT.*

MATTE: A mask which obstructs some of the light passing through the camera lens. It can be of a specific shape (e.g. a keyhole) which is imposed on the film as a blank area while the photographic images are being exposed. In silent days it was often left blank. Nowadays mattes are more often produced with laboratory techniques than with camera-mounted masks. See *TRAVELING MATTE.*

MEDIUM SHOT: See *SHOT.*

MISE-EN-SCÈNE: A term generally used in reference to the staging of a play or a film production—in considering as a whole the settings, the arrangements of the actors in relation to the setting, lighting, etc. Some critics use the concept of mise-en-scène to describe what goes on within the frame in contrast with cutting, as the key approaches to filmmakers' styles.

MONTAGE: In Russia, montage meant *DYNAMIC CUTTING;* in Europe, the term is equivalent to editing; in Hollywood, it is used more specifically to describe a sequence using rapid *SUPERIMPOSITIONS, JUMP-CUTS,* and *DISSOLVES* in order to create a kind of kaleidoscopic effect.

MOVING SHOT: See *SHOT.*

OPTICALS: SPECIAL EFFECTS usually created in the laboratory with an optical printer, but most of them can also be created in the camera. These include most *TRANSITIONS* (dissolve, fade, iris, wipe). See, for example, *MATTE, SUPERIMPOSITION,* and *TRAVELING MATTE.*

PAN SHOT: See *SHOT.*

PARALLEL ACTION: An effect created by *CROSS-CUTTING,* which enables the viewer to be two or more places concurrently. Using parallel action, a filmmaker can extend or condense *REAL TIME* and create a *SCREEN TIME* with a logic of its own. For instance, if the filmmaker wants to lengthen the suspense while the heroine has one minute to answer a question on a TV quiz show, he can cut between the homes of anxious friends watching in four different cities.

REACTION SHOT: A *CUTAWAY* shot of a person reacting to the main action as listener or spectator. Some comedians have planned reaction shots to jokes in order to give the audience a chance to laugh without missing the next line.

REAL TIME: The actual time an action would need to occur; as opposed to *screen time,* a principal aesthetic effect created by filmmakers in transforming reality into art. Real time is preserved within the scenes of a play but (usually) only within the individual shots of a film.

REAR PROJECTION: A technique whereby the actors, sets, and props in front of the camera are combined with a background which consists of a translucent screen on which a picture (moving or still) is projected from behind. Almost always used when a scene takes place inside a moving vehicle. The actors sit still and the scenery they are supposedly passing by is projected behind them. Sometimes called *back projection* or *process shot.*

REVERSE-ANGLE SHOT: See *SHOT.*

SCENE: See *UNITS OF FILM LENGTH.*

SCREEN DIRECTION: Whichever direction, left or right, the actor or object is looking at or moving toward, described from the *audience point of view.*

SCREEN TIME: Duration of an action as manipulated through editing, as opposed to *REAL TIME.* A principal aesthetic effect by which the filmmaker transforms reality into art. *CUTAWAYS* and *INSERT SHOTS* are two ways of stretching or condensing real time to give the film different time. If we cut between a race and the spectators' reactions, we often lengthen the actual time of the race. If we cut away for part of a movement, when we cut back we may

have cut out a large chunk of the action. For other ways of manipulating time see: *FAST* and *SLOW MOTION, CROSS-CUTTING, HIDDEN CUT, JUMP-CUTS,* and *PARALLEL ACTION.*

SEPARATION: Shooting people in separate shots who are actually quite close together. A conversation may be filmed with one person looking right in *MEDIUM SHOT* and the other looking left in *CLOSE-UP* (probably after a two-shot establishing their nearness). A unique tool of cinema which can bring people in closer relation than if they were in the same shot.

SEQUENCE: See *UNITS OF FILM LENGTH.*

SHOT: A piece of film that has been exposed, without cuts or interruptions, in a single running of the camera. The shot is the elemental division of a film. Shots may be categorized:

According to the *distance* between the camera and its subject—these designations vary among directors and are relative to the size of the subject filmed and the way distances have been established in the film:

- *LONG SHOT* (LS): The camera seems to be at a distance from the subject being filmed.
- *MEDIUM SHOT (MS):* A shot intermediate in distance between a long and a close shot.
- *CLOSE-UP (CU):* The camera seems very close to the subject, so that when the image is projected most of the screen will be taken up with revealing a face and its expressions, or a plate of stew.
- *EXTREME CLOSE-UP (ECU):* The camera seems very close to what would ordinarily be a mere detail in a close-up. For example, the whole screen is taken up with a shot of a tear welling up in an eye.

According to the *angle* of the camera in relation to the subject:

- *HIGH-ANGLE SHOT:* A shot which looks down on the subject from a height.
- *LOW-ANGLE SHOT:* A shot which looks up at the subject.
- *EYE-LEVEL SHOT:* Guess.
- *REVERSE-ANGLE SHOT:* Shot taken by a camera positioned opposite (about 180°) from where the previous shot

was taken. A reverse angle of a dog walking toward the camera would be a shot of it walking directly away from the camera. If a reverse-angle is made of two people in a *TWO-SHOT,* the rules of *CROSSING THE AXIS* have to be observed by reversing their position.

According to the *content,* nature or subject matter of what is being filmed:

- *ESTABLISHING SHOT:* Often the opening shot of a sequence, showing the location of a scene or the arrangement of its characters. Usually a *LONG SHOT.* For example, if the story jumps from lover's lane, where an athlete is breaking training on the night before the big game, to his disastrous fumble at the championship, we will probably see the stadium and teams from a *HIGH-ANGLE LONG SHOT* before we close in on the hero's actions. Compare *SLOW DISCLOSURE.*
- *MASTER SHOT:* Single shot of an entire piece of dramatic action. A standard Hollywood practice that facilitates the editing of a scene. For example, a conversation is likely to be photographed first as one lengthy *TWO-SHOT;* then it will be reshot in pieces at the different distances and angles needed to construct the scene.
- *TWO-SHOT:* Two persons in the same frame.
- *THREE-SHOT:* Three persons in the same frame.

Or according to the *means* by which the shot is accomplished physically:

- *CIRCULAR CAMERA MOVEMENT:* A camera movement that travels around its more or less stationary subject.
- *DOLLY* or *TRACKING SHOT*: one in which the camera moves bodily from one place to another. (Compare *PAN* and *TRACKING SHOTS.*)
- *MOVING SHOT:* One taken which the camera stays in one place but rotates horizontally on its axis.
- *SWISH PAN:* A pan so rapid that the image appears blurred. It usually begins and ends at rest.
- *TILT SHOT:* One in which the camera pivots along a

vertical plane.

- *TRACKING SHOT:* A dolly shot in which the camera moves parallel with its moving subject. If the camera moves in on a seated person, that is a dolly-in; if it travels alongside of a person walking down the block, that is a tracking shot.
- *ZOOM SHOT:* A shot taken with a zoom lens (i.e., a lens which makes it possible to move visually toward or away from a subject without moving the camera). We can get closer to a subject with either a dolly or zoom shot. When we dolly into a subject, objects pass by the camera, giving a feeling of depth. When we zoom, the sensation is two-dimensional, much like coming close to a still photograph. Zooms are used a lot in covering football games.

SLOW DISCLOSURE: A shot starting in *CLOSE-UP* that does not reveal the location of the subject at first. It then moves back or cuts to a full revelation of the geography, which comes as a surprise. A shot typical of cartoons would show an animal sleeping comfortably and then zoom out to reveal that his enemy is lowering an axe over his head.

SLOW MOTION: Opposite of *FAST MOTION.* The action appears slower on the screen than it could in reality. Popular for dream and romantic effects, and to show the gracefulness of athletes.

SOFT FOCUS: See *FOCUS.*

SPECIAL EFFECTS: Visual special effects are *OPTICALS.*

STOCK FOOTAGE: Footage borrowed from previous films or a stock library. It is often newsreel footage of famous people and events or battle scenes and other hard to shoot footage.

STOP MOTION: The method by which trick photography is effected; the film is exposed one frame at a time, allowing time for rearrangement of models, etc., between shots and thus giving the illusion of motion by something normally inanimate. This is how King Kong was filmed and also how flowers can grow, bloom, and die within a few minutes. Stop motion applied to objects is animation, applied to people is pixilation.

SUBJECTIVE SHOT: Shot that seems to represent the point of view of a character in the story. It may be what he sees (e.g., a shot

through the keyhole he is peeking through into the next room), or how he sees it (e.g., a blurred shot looking up at the surgeon from the operating table as the character awakes from anaesthesia). In *The Cabinet of Dr. Caligari,* we learn at the end of the film that the distorted, *EXPRESSIONISTIC MISE-EN-SCÈNE* reflects the fact that the film's narrator is a mental patient.

SUPERIMPOSITION: An *OPTICAL* effect in which two or more images are on one piece of film, so that there appears to be a multiple exposure. Can be used when two characters played by the same actor have to meet; also for dissolves, dream sequences, etc.

SWISH PAN: see *SHOT.*

SYNC or *SYNCHRONISM:* The relation between picture and sound. If they don't match, the film is said to be "out of sync." Easiest to spot by watching a person's lips as he speaks.

TAKE: See *UNITS OF FILM LENGTH.*

THREE-SHOT: See *SHOT.*

TILT SHOT: See *SHOT.*

TRACKING SHOT: see *SHOT.*

TRANSITIONS: Means of connecting two shots. The following transitions can be created either in the laboratory with an optical printer or in the camera.

- *DISSOLVE:* The merging of the end of one shot with the beginning of the next; as the second shot becomes distinct, the first slowly fades away. Thus, for a while two images are *SUPERIMPOSED.* Also called *lap dissolves* and, in England, *mixes.*
- *FADE:* A fade-in shot begins in darkness and gradually assumes full brightness. A fade-out shot gradually gets darker.
- *IRIS:* An iris-in shot opens from darkness into an expanding circle within which is the image. An iris-out is the opposite.
- *WIPE:* A transition in which the second shot appears and "pushes" off the first one; usually they are separated by a visible vertical line, but the variations of wipes are many. Unlike an iris, there is a picture on both sides of the dividing line.

TRAVELING MATTE: A *SPECIAL EFFECT* used to blend actors in the studio with location or trick scenes. The actor is photographed against a dark background and this image can later be com-

bined optically with the desired background. Thus actors can move among animated monsters, exploding shells, or cobras. The traveling matte is therefore unlike *REAR PROJECTION.*

TWO-SHOT: See *SHOT.*

UNITS OF FILM LENGTH:

- *FRAME:* The individual picture on a strip of film. Sound films project 24 frames per second.
- *SHOT:* A piece of film that has been exposed without cuts or interruptions. (Defined in detail under its own alphabetical listing.)
- *TAKE:* Each performance of a piece of action in front of a camera (from "lights, camera, action!" to "cut!"). Each recording is numbered sequentially, until the director feels he has satisfactory results. From the takes he chooses one for each shot.
- *SCENE AND SEQUENCE:* Although the terms are used constantly, there is no agreement on what these units comprise. One definition is that a scene is determined by unity of time and place (like a dramatic scene) whereas a sequence is determined by unity of action (a more filmic unit).

WIPE: See *TRANSITIONS.*

ZOOM SHOT: See *SHOT.*

1040